The Climbing Garden

The Climbing Garden

Cathy Wilkinson Barash

Director, Garden Writers
Association of America

FRIEDMAN/FAIRFAX
PUBLISHERS

A FRIEDMAN/FAIRFAX BOOK

Copyright © 2000, 1997 by Michael Friedman Publishing Group, Inc.

Previously published as *Vines & Climbers*.

Library of Congress Cataloging-in-Publication Data available upon request.

ISBN 1-56799-964-6

Editor: Nathaniel Marunas
Art Director: Lynne Yeamans
Designer: Andrea Karman
Photography Editor: Deborah Bernhardt

Color separations by Colourscan Overseas Co., Pte Ltd.
Printed in China by Leefung-Asco Printers Ltd.

3 5 7 9 10 8 6 4 2

For bulk purchases and special sales, please contact:
Friedman/Fairfax Publishers
Attention: Sales Department
15 West 26th Street
New York, New York 10010
212/685-6610   FAX 212/685-1307

Visit our website:
http://www.metrobooks.com

PHOTOGRAPHY CREDITS

©Cathy Wilkinson Barash: pp. 54, 56, 62, 65, 68, 87, 105, 115; ©Crandall and Crandall: p. 79; ©Ken Druse: pp. 1
background, 3 background, 36, 77, 92, 107; ©Derek Fell: pp. 10, 28 top, 42 bottom, 46, 48, 51, 64, 73, 91; ©John Glover: pp.
14, 21 bottom, 26 bottom, 28 bottom, 33, 39, 42 top, 43 left, 49, 57, 81, 88, 93, 98; ©Dency Kane: pp. 17 top, 24-25,
26 top, 31 chart background, 33 chart background, 34, 35, 37 both, 41 chart background, 47, 55, 58, 67, 70, 72, 78,
106, 113; ©Allan Mandell: pp. 9, 43 right, 116; ©Charles Mann: pp. 6 background and inset, 7 background, 11, 15, 17 bottom,
19, 20, 45, 82, 85, 101, 108–9, 111, 112, 114; Jennifer S. Markson (garden illustrations): pp. 117, 118 both, 119,
120 both, 121, 122 both, 123 both, 124–125; ©Clive Nichols: pp. 1 inset, 12, 13, 21 top, 22, 27, 29, 30, 44, 50, 60,
89, 96–97, 103; ©Graham Strong: pp. 8; Designer: Jill Billington: p. 13; P. Crawshaw: p. 89; M. Walker: p. 44; ©Jerry Pavia:
pp. 53, 71, 90, 110; ©Richard Shiell: pp. 2, 16, 32, 52, 59, 61, 69, 74, 75, 80, 83, 86, 94–95, 100, 102

Dedication

To Rizz Arthur Dean

Acknowledgments

My heartfelt thanks go to the many people who worked behind the scenes—their efforts, as always, were above and beyond the call of duty.

- Christina Ward, agent extraordinaire, who is always there for me (or at least her answering machine is)

- Nathaniel Marunas, my editor at Michael Friedman

- Christina and Ida Norden, enthusiastic proofreaders and trellis builders

- Rosemary Fasulo and Elisa Robinson, whose assistance keeps the photos in some semblance of order

- Andy Durbridge, Christina Norden, Betty Pruehsner, and Elisa Robinson, garden designers

- Barbara and all the folks at Jomark, who always rush my slides with a smile

- And most of all, my cat Sebastian, who helps in the garden, supervises the office, and, most importantly, is my constant loving companion

Table of Contents

Looking Up

INTRODUCTION

Vines and climbers have been a part of my gardening experience since childhood. My family's first house was in Point Lookout, a small beach town on Long Island. No one had much property, and back in the early 1950s, we were one of the few families who lived there year-round. Yards were tiny, with most of the available space taken up by patios. At the far end of our concrete patio there was a small, raised-bed garden, two feet (61cm) deep and fifteen or twenty feet (4.6–6.1m) long. A three-foot-high (91.4cm) white brick wall marked both the back of the garden and the property boundary. A white lattice rose five or six feet (1.5–1.8m) above the brick wall. In that small space, we grew tomatoes, morning glories, and climbing roses, all trained upward. One year I remember there were even some small melon and cucumber vines twining up the trellis. Low-growing annual flowers were tucked in among the other plants, providing colorful accents. A honeysuckle plant thrived in one corner, climbing out of the garden and thrusting itself up onto the garage. Only in winter, when the garden was dormant, could we see through the lattice to the neighbor's yard. On long summer evenings, the contrast of the dark plants against the white lattice made the garden a thing of mystical beauty, especially after the sun went down. Over the last twenty-five years I have lived in different parts of the United States, and, for a short time, in Portugal. In each of my gardens, I have made use of vines and climbers. They have proved their versatility over and over—as privacy screens, to maximize gardening in a small space, for erosion control on a hillside—but I have planted them always and especially for their beauty.

THE VERSATILITY OF VINES AND CLIMBERS

No matter how large or small your garden may be, you can improve it by including vines and climbers. First and foremost, they maximize growing space in any garden. Plants growing upward do not take up valuable square footage on the ground for anything but their stems and roots. Growing plants vertically offers other practical advantages, too. The increased air circulation around the plants lessens the chance that they will suffer from fungus and disease. When plants grow upward, more leaves are exposed to the sunlight, usually resulting in healthier, happier plants.

Vines and climbers have a wide range of uses in the landscape. They can soften stark architectural lines, conceal unattractive portions of the hardscape (such as fences or walls), provide a screen for shade and/or privacy, create barriers, and as already mentioned, extend limited garden space. Don't overlook the fact that they can move the focal point up above eye level. Elegant foliage, flowers, or fruit grow in front of and above the onlooker, drawing the eye upward. Believe it or not, this adds considerable interest to the garden. Some vines that you may be accustomed to think of as ground covers, such as euonymus and ivies, are wonderful when trained to grow skyward; others, such as Virginia creeper, climb naturally without any assistance. Furthermore, in addition to growing up, vines can also grow downward when planted in containers up off the ground, in hanging baskets and windowboxes, for example. They soften the edges of containers, yet they can give a nice vertical line to container plantings. Some vines, like climbing hydrangea and wisteria, can create a focal point in the landscape; to make the most of this effect, set the vine off by itself, and use it as a specimen plant so it gets all the attention it deserves without competition from other plants.

PAGE 8: *Passiflora caerulea* growing through *Lonicera nitida* 'Baggesin's Gold'.

PAGE 9: All the flowers on a Chinese wisteria bloom at the same time.

OPPOSITE: Winter creeper *(Euonymus fortunei)* climbs a stone wall, pruned to resemble an espaliered tree.

LEFT: *Actinidia kolomikta* is striking, with its pink- and cream-tipped leaves.

HOW PLANTS CLIMB

Vines and climbers are winners in the ongoing evolutionary battle that results, as Darwin described, in the survival of the fittest. Where competition for room to grow, nutrients, and light—so necessary for photosynthesis—is fierce, vines literally climbed out of the morass of ground-dwelling plants, lengthened their stems, and grew up into the sunlight, often using their competition as support in their upward journey. Vines are not genetically constrained, as trees and shrubs are, to a prescribed form. They can fit into the tiniest space, provided their roots are firmly anchored in the soil, and grow vertically and/or horizontally even among dense vegetation.

Unlike many other plants, vines grow in no predetermined fashion; they are flexible and, left to their own devices, take whatever route will provide them with adequate sunlight. Scientifically speaking, vines and climbers are strongly phototropic: they grow toward light. Many in fact are positively heliotropic: the movement of their stems, shoots, or leaves is influenced not only by light, but also by the movement of the sun. Additionally, sweet peas and some other vines are thigmotropic: their tendrils respond to physical contact, causing them to twine around a support when they touch one.

For simplicity's sake, vines may be divided into two basic types: clinging and nonclinging. Clinging vines can attach themselves physically to almost any surface by one of various means. Boston ivy, for example, has short tendrils with disklike suction cups at the ends, and these allow it to attach itself to even smooth surfaces. Climbing hydrangea, English ivy, creeping fig, wintercreeper, and trumpet vine attach themselves with small, rootlike hold-fasts along their stems. They thrive when provided with slightly rough surfaces, such as brick, wood, or stone, to grow up. An unsightly chain-link fence can be hidden attractively and in relatively little time (a few seasons) by a combination of ivy or wintercreeper (both evergreen, so the fence looks nice in winter) and trumpet vine (for color and attracting hummingbirds in summer).

Nonclinging vines have several distinct growth habits that enable them to climb. Twining vines spiral upward around a support. This spiraling motion, technically called circumnutation, may be clockwise or counterclockwise. Most often the spiral path is at a right angle to a light or heat source. It is interesting to note that twining vines are naturally programmed to twine either clockwise or counterclockwise. Many times I have inadvertently wound a vine around a support stake only to come back to the garden an hour later to find it on the ground. Vines will unwind themselves and then rewind so they are twining in the direction that is correct for them. If you take a hanging basket of morning glories that has stakes in it to train the plant upward and turn the whole thing upside–down, the vines will uncoil themselves and then retwine so that they are properly oriented. Observe your plants and note the direction in which they twine. Chinese wisteria twines from left to right, whereas Japanese wisteria twines from right to left.

It is not only a twining stem that supports vines, but other appendages too. With some plants, such as peas and sweet peas, the leaves or parts of the leaves are transformed into slender tough threads, called tendrils, that corkscrew around supports. Cucurbits and passion flowers have tendrils that grow from the leaf axils and are commonly considered modified branches. Grape tendrils, also modified branches, may in time become woody, and then are called vine tendrils.

The last group of nonclinging vines are best described as scramblers. These plants, which include climbing roses, are not vines in the true sense of the word, as they have no means of keeping themselves upright. However, they grow distinctively long stems. They require support to keep them vertical, and loose ties or some similar means are often used to keep them secured to their support. There are many plants that combine several techniques for righting themselves. For example, jasmine is a scrambler with a partially twining habit. Whatever means they use to pull themselves upward or along the ground, vines and climbers are ingeniously adapted to help you make the most of any garden space.

OPPOSITE: A venerable Boston ivy (*Parthenocissus tricuspidata*) in autumnal splendor climbs the stone cloisters.

RIGHT: Variegated ivy lightens the background and draws the eye to the trellis, while the grapes above are supported by a pergola.

The Supporting Players

In any production, the supporting actors play a vital role, although they are sometimes underappreciated, given their contribution. With vines and climbers, one or more elements of the hardscape are the supporting actors. In essence, hardscape is the nonliving backbone of a garden—the bones of the garden that are visible even before plants are added. The hardscape is visible in winter when most plants are dormant. For vines and climbers, the significant portions of the hardscape to consider include any wall, fence, trellis, arbor, arch, pergola, gazebo, and the walls of a structure (house, garage, barn, even doghouse). In addition to these permanent, virtually nonmovable parts of the landscape, consider also the conventional and smaller-scale supports that are easily added or taken away as needed: cages, stakes, tepees, wires, and netting.

COLOR IN THE HARDSCAPE

It is purely a matter of personal preference whether these structural components become more than just a physical foundation for plantings. No matter how large or small a support may be, color plays a vital role in how the hardscape combines with the rest of the garden. Left in their natural state, wooden structures tend to blend into the background. Even a large wooden gazebo that has weathered for several years is less intrusive on the landscape than a painted structure. Robert Dash, a well-known contemporary painter and gardener, uses vivid colors throughout the hardscape of his Long Island garden, Madoo. His use of color is bold and unexpected, from a bright red-orange bridge in the midst of a cool, woodland garden to a chartreuse bench (fashioned wheelbarrow-style with a metal wheel at one end and handles at the other). A lilac-colored gazebo tends to grab your attention, luring you into that portion of the garden; the gazebo, a loud exclamation point, proves to be a lovely foil for the green leaves of the vines that climb up it. It draws your attention more to the shape of the plant than if the gazebo were painted a dark earth tone. Dark, naturalistic colors are good for setting off variegated foliage and light-colored flowers, especially at night.

Color has a major effect on the garden impact, both by day and by night. Before you decide to paint (or not to paint) the components of your hardscape, ask yourself some questions. Is the structure attractive? You may want to show off a handsome trellis by painting it a bright or light, attention-getting color. A chain-link fence by itself is quite ugly, yet would become nearly invisible when painted dark green or dark brown with a lovely vine weaving itself through the links.

Ask yourself what time of day you'll spend the most time looking at each part of the garden. Choose whatever colors you like, and they will show up well (or fade into the background, whichever you wish) in the daytime. If you want to enjoy the garden at night, you need to consider what colors are most visible in a limited light. Without the enhancement of garden lighting, white has the most impact in the dark. Light and pale colors rank next, followed by clear bright yellows and pinks. Finally, reds disappear almost completely, even in the light of a full moon, and dark colors fade into the gloom.

Do you want to enhance your garden with lighting? You can add artificial lighting to your garden for a dramatic nighttime effect. Use lighting judiciously. Never highlight or spotlight more than three plants or structures in a typical backyard garden, because the result will look too busy. Stay away from the "runway" effect, rows of yellow or orange lights lining a driveway or path. Avoid using masses of brightly colored

PAGE 14: A climbing hydrangea in spring bloom easily scales a wall.

PAGE 15: Morning glory romps through an ancient sundial.

RIGHT: The bright orange flowers of black-eyed Susan vine set off its velvety black centers. Enjoy the flowers of this vine outdoors from spring until the first frost, and indoors throughout the winter.

TOP: A 'Meidiland White' rose brightens a wall, giving the illusion that the plant is spilling down and over, when it is actually trained upwards.

BOTTOM: The luscious pink flowers and prominent yellow stamens of *Lonicera sempervirens* are set off by the round green leaves.

lights—reserve them for the holidays. Before making any lighting feature permanent, try it out and view it from all angles. I once visited a garden with a gorgeous white gazebo, large enough so that six of us had dinner inside it, gazing out into the garden. When it had grown completely dark, the host flicked a switch on one of the posts of the gazebo to illuminate the garden for us. Instead, it was we who were lit up. We felt as though we were performers in a theater-in-the-round, with spotlights and footlights aimed up at us from all sides. The lighting designer had used a dramatic lighting technique, called uplighting, wherein lights at ground level were aimed upward to illuminate the eight posts of the gazebo. Indeed, it looked spectacular when viewed from a distance, but from inside the gazebo, unfortunately, the effect was blinding.

What will be the color of the flowers that will eventually climb on the structure? In theory it may sound like a good idea to paint the supporting structure the same color as the flowers, but this rarely works. I once painted a small rose arbor red. I had even gone to the trouble of bringing a rose to the paint store to match its color with the paint chips. In doing this, I made two major mistakes: first, in matching colors in the store, and second, in trying to second-guess Mother Nature. Always view paint chips in the light in which the painted object will be seen. The light in paint stores is often fluorescent, which has a cool, blue cast—very unlike the warm, full-spectrum light of the sun. Even if I had not made that first mistake, I soon realized that each rose blossom is not exactly the same color. Although a few matched the arbor perfectly, most clashed with its bright color. Those that did match its color seemed to almost disappear, because the eye perceived them as merely part of the background.

Use bright colors carefully and in small amounts for bold contrasts. Rosalind Creasy, a landscape designer, garden writer, and photographer in northern California, always impresses me with her unique, front-yard edible landscapes. One year she erected an eye-catching, cobalt-blue trellis with orange-flowered nasturtiums climbing up it and lavender planted at its base. I thought it was gorgeous. You, however, might not be comfortable with such bold colors in your own garden. Use whatever colors you like. Be creative. You may want to experiment with a small support, even something as modest as a tomato stake. Be adventuresome and paint it blue, or yellow, or orange; you may find you enjoy the bright colors. If you don't like it, you can easily repaint it an unobtrusive green or brown.

When your vine is fully grown (or at the size you plan to keep it trained), how much of the structure will you be able to see? Consider how much you *want* to see. An old, ugly, waist-high concrete wall in my garden was a real eyesore. Yet, it made a practical home for my houseplants in summer. For camouflage, I planted bird's-foot ivy on both sides of the wall, spacing the plants eight inches (20.3cm) apart, and within a year and a half the wall was covered. Now, at a quick glance, it looks as though the potted plants are floating in the middle of the garden, because the green wall blends in with the rest of the foliage. Some vines grow at prodigious rates, a point of concern when considering planting next to a building. Train the vine away from areas you want clear, especially windows and doorways. Keep up with your vines; since they grow up more often than out, the tendency is to forget about them until suddenly the third-storey window has disappeared in a tangle of Boston ivy. (When that happens, it may be easier to prune from indoors, rather than trying to balance on a very tall ladder.)

Contrast, whether it be bold or subtle, is necessary. I recall a lovely old wisteria that grew in a friend's yard, trained up a broad white trellis situated a few feet in front of a dark green shed. I visited when the wisteria was in full bloom, but it was difficult to appreciate it. The white flowers were indistinguishable from the white trellis except when viewed from close up. Those blossoms that grew away from the trellis showed up magnificently against the dark green shed. Had either the wisteria or the trellis been a deeper color, it all would have worked much more satisfactorily.

THE RIGHT STUFF

Pair the right plant with the right support. I have not followed that simple rule more times than I care to admit. It sounds so basic, and indeed is so important, yet it is often overlooked or ignored. I am sure I am not the only person who has put a large tomato cage around a determinate tomato that will grow only three feet (91.4cm) high. The tomatoes on the entire plant will ripen at the same time, and the plant will finish producing by the first of August; that isn't a terrible mistake, but it is overkill—overutilization of support. I also admit I have planted an indeterminate tomato, such as 'Sweet 100', with a six-foot (1.8m) bamboo stake (with about a quarter of the stake's length below ground) for support; having tied the plant loosely to the stake, I felt smug that I had supported it well. Three weeks later, I see the stake careening off at a odd angle (that is, when I'm lucky; often the stake is on the ground) with stems of the plant broken, and the tomato heading off six feet (1.8m) in every direction. *That* was the plant that should have been put in a strong, tall cage, or at least staked with a 2-by-4.

So do a little research before putting up a support or buying that pretty little vine in a one-gallon (3.8L) pot from a mail-order catalog. Find out how large the plant you covet will grow before bringing it home. A friend of mine has one of the most magnificent climbing hydrangeas I have ever seen, and it

This sturdy wooden arbor holds lovely white wisteria blossoms aloft. Be sure to make the arbor tall enough to allow ample space for walking through when plants are in bloom.

is at least twenty-five years old. It was originally planted at the base of an old oak tree with the idea that the oak would provide support for the hydrangea. After a number of years, my friend noticed that the tree was beginning to list to one side. A quick consultation with an arborist defined the problem. The hydrangea was climbing up only one side of the tree, weighing it down. Seeing how healthy both the oak and hydrangea were, the arborist attached several guy wires to the opposite side of the tree, pulling it back to vertical, and preventing it from

leaning again. Today the hydrangea soars a good thirty or more feet (9m) into the air, and when it is in bloom high in the branches of the oak tree the effect is majestic.

It is always worth the investment to use quality material, especially for large support structures. Do-it-yourself is fine, as long as you know what you are doing and use the proper materials. Several years ago I built an arbor from four inexpensive pieces of lattice. I nailed the lattices together, placed the arbor over a walkway of thyme in my edible flower garden, planted scarlet runner bean seeds on both sides of the arbor, watered them, and watched them grow. It looked magnificent with the vines growing across the top of the arbor and brilliant scarlet flowers and luscious beans hanging down from heart-shaped leaves. However, the south side of the arbor got much more sun than the north side. The vines with the southern exposure were more prolific, and soon the joints at the top of the arbor began to give way beneath the weight of the vines. I rigged a solution by securing adjoining sections of lattice together with twist-ties. They held it well until a night several weeks later when there was a violent thunderstorm. In the morning when I went outdoors, I saw disaster. The arbor had fallen over and broken into pieces. That was when I realized another mistake: I had not anchored the arbor in the ground. If I had simply attached tomato stakes to the arbor and sunk them eighteen to twenty-four inches (45.7–61cm) into the ground, my arbor might have made it through the season. A support cannot be anchored *too* deeply.

Before planting an annual vine with tendrils, make sure the support lends itself to easy removal of the dead vine in fall or winter. I have unwittingly torn apart several wooden trellises when trying to pull down moonflower vines in late fall. Their tendrils, even when the rest of the plant is dead and brittle, hang tenaciously onto their support. In some cases it is best to cut the strong tendrils with pruners to release the plant.

WALLS

It is tempting to use the walls of the house as supports for vines and climbers. A white or light color usually works best as a vertical background, particularly if you want to see the shape of the plants, especially at night. However, you may not have a choice about the background. Assume that the garden abuts a dark-colored house, and you want to grow some vines against

OPPOSITE: *Clematis montana* scales this wall with the aid of nearly invisible support—wires inobtrusively strung across the upper portion of the wall.

TOP: A bright blue door and yellow walls set the stage for brilliant fall hues—scarlet Boston ivy (*Parthenocissus tricuspidata*) and the changing hues of *Vitis coignetiae.*

BOTTOM: *Hedera colchica* 'Destatde Variegata' spills up and over this wooden fence, adding a touch of warmth to a plain outdoor structure.

the house. It would look quite strange to paint one side or just a portion of a wall of the house white just so the vines would show to good advantage. An alternative solution is to erect a white or light-colored natural wood trellis at least six inches (15.2cm) in front of the wall and use that for training your plants. It adds a new dimension to the architecture, while the contrast between the light tone of the trellis and the blackness of the space behind gives a sense of depth. Be sure not to let the plants cover the trellis completely, or you will lose the intended effect.

If you are planning to use the wall of a building as a support, consider types of climbers and how they attach themselves. Clinging vines are easiest to use against a wall. Ivy looks beautiful growing up a brick wall—it calls up images of rustic New England towns and villages. However, the rootlike hold-fasts that allow ivy to grow vertically so easily can work their way into old or soft masonry, weakening the mortar that holds the bricks or stones together. Tear down the ivy and the venerable institutions of New England might come tumbling down too. A better choice for a building constructed with mortar is Boston ivy, which climbs with disklike suction cups that hold on without damaging the surface. Avoid planting such aggressive vines as wisteria next to wooden buildings, as the plant can ease itself between the clapboards, causing extensive damage. It can also wreak havoc with the roof, working itself through the shingles, eventually leading to water damage. At Sooke Harbour House in British Columbia, I saw a lovely nasturtium flowering in the dining room. The only problem was that it was flowering against the inside wall, having crept in from outdoors. Even the mildest-mannered plants can become aggressive given the right conditions.

Walls, whether high or low, are great supports for the right vine. A low wall can be used as a support for winter creeper,

Wisteria floribunda 'Multijuga' is trained to elegantly overhang this stately wooden door. Prune the wisteria after it finishes blooming to keep the vine from running out of bounds.

and with a trellis or lattice mounted behind such a wall, a cucumber can twine up high. Remember that twining vines need more than a flat surface; they need three-dimensional support to wrap their stems or tendrils around. With some mortar nails, fasten a length of bird netting to a concrete or brick wall, and morning glory can wind its way up any wall, greeting the day with its showy flowers. Check local nurseries, garden centers, and mail-order catalogs for the latest gadgets that allow nonclinging vines to scale a flat surface. Nail-in and stick-on clasps can adhere to most surfaces; enough of these clasps (and a little training) will hold a beautiful annual vine such as canary creeper aloft all summer long. Hinge a lattice or trellis to a wall with a strong hook and eye. This is an excellent method for instant, effective support for annual vines that can be removed easily in winter, and the support is moved easily if you need to paint the wall. The simplest method for allowing twining vines to scale a wall is to secure stout string or twine to the top of (or above) the wall, and let the vine go. Be sure to anchor the string into the soil so a strong wind does not whip the plant out of the ground.

TRELLISES

A trellis, by strict definition, is a structure of intersecting narrow strips with square open spaces in between. It is used as a support for plants or as a screen, and it is made of wood or plastic. As mentioned above, a trellis is useful for transforming a dark wall. A trellis is rarely freestanding, especially if used for support. Nailed top and bottom to strong pieces of wood, and anchored well into the ground, a trellis can support most annual vines. A tall trellis is often used as part of an attractive pergola.

Straying from the strict definition is a fan trellis. This is constructed usually from three or five long strips of wood, bound together at the bottom for a length of at least eight inches (20.3cm), and two or three crosspieces of wood with holes drilled in them so the wood strips can fit through them. The crosspieces are set so the verticals splay out to form an attractive fan shape. Fan trellises are commonly placed near or against a wall, with the lower portion inserted into the ground. I have successfully used fan trellises in tall, narrow pots planted with moonflowers. Placed in front of the windows in my sunroom, the effect was that of a living awning that cooled the sunroom in the daytime and filled it with the heavenly perfume of the moonflowers at night.

Coming back into fashion are hand-crafted, bentwood trellises. They are available through some mail-order garden catalogs and at nurseries and specialty shops. In some areas of the country, they are sold at rural farm stands. If you have the time and the right wood, you can easily make one yourself in a few hours. I took a trellis-making workshop at Peconic River Herb Farm on Long Island and was amazed at what I created in a short time. Using hardwood for the uprights and softer pieces of wood for the major crosspieces, I nailed the basic form together. The artistic touch comes with the pliable, green wood of the vines. There are many wild vines free for the taking. Wisteria, honeysuckle, wild grape, porcelainberry, and Virginia creeper are easily found in my neck of the woods. Be careful not to use poison ivy—the results could be disastrous. The vines are bent and nailed into place (for a more naturalistic look, you can lash them with narrow vines or reeds) to create a curved design—heart-shaped, curlicued, swirled, and so on. The result of my first efforts was sturdy enough to support a large squash plant grown in a whiskey barrel.

FENCES AND GATES

Unlike a trellis, a fence is usually self-supporting. Although lower than a trellis, a fence can nonetheless add an interesting vertical line to an otherwise flat garden, while providing support for vines and climbers. A fence need not surround the entire garden; it may be used to set off a portion of the garden picture. An unusual use of fencing is to bridge two living vertical elements in a garden, such as two sections of a hedge. Fencing can play an integral role in the garden but, depending on its form and function, you may not want to feature it. For example, a metal deer fence acts as a security barrier between the hungry deer and the delicious plants in the garden. It is functional but unattractive, not something you want as a focal point necessarily. However, you can improve it and achieve a rustic look by planting morning glories along the fence. The deer will not eat the poisonous plants, and the morning glory flowers will beautify the garden border from late spring until a killing frost. Once you plant morning glories, they usually reseed if the ground is undisturbed. The beauty of these plants will last for many summers.

Fences come in a wide array of shapes, sizes, heights, and materials. The style of the fence can help set the tone of the garden. A low, white picket fence conjures up images of a cottage garden, especially with sweet peas climbing about the fence in late spring. Bamboo, split and bent to form U-shapes, makes a simple, low barrier for a Japanese-influenced garden. Train a variegated ivy along the U-shapes for a unique effect. A split-rail fence is a fine border for a rambling, rustic garden or for edging a large horse farm or estate. I have a large sweet autumn clematis that sprawls along a split-rail fence, adding a touch of class with its ethereal beauty and fragrance in September. A low, wrought-iron fence with climbing nasturtiums makes a great border for a formal herb garden.

A tumble of roses in this Atlanta, Georgia, garden looks cool and inviting. Twining up the arbor as a backdrop as well as growing up a fence, 'Eden' is the featured rose in this setting.

Fences are natural foils for gates. A gate allows you passage from one side of the fence to the other, without the nuisance of having to jump the fence. Perhaps even more than the fences themselves, the gates set a mood. A white picket fence need not have a plain white picket gate. The gate might be ornate, a sort of gingerbread effect. Or the gate might have pickets, but with the top cut in a half-moon shape. The gate could sport an arbor of pink roses arching above it. Finally, a gate need not be connected to a fence. Old wrought-iron gates make interesting art objects in the garden, while providing support for edible vines such as cucumbers and peas.

ARBORS AND PERGOLAS

By definition, an arbor is a roofless tunnel-like passage shaded by vines growing up latticework on either side. A pergola is also an arbor, but with an open roof of cross rafters or latticework supported on posts or columns, usually covered with climbing vines. The difference between the two is the placement of the latticework. For an arbor, the latticework forms the sides; for a pergola, columns or posts support a latticework "roof." A pergola is more effective support for a plant that has a long stem and a heavy vining habit, such as wisteria, trumpet vine, or grapes. An arbor works well for a plant with abundant foliage and flowers along the stems, such as roses, moonflower, or honeysuckle. An arbor usually has straight sides and a convex top, while a pergola is formed of right angles. As to size, an arbor may be only two or three feet (61–91.4cm) deep, spanning a garden gate. Often several arbors are arranged in sequence to form a long bower; separated by eight to ten feet (2.4–3m), such a series can give the feeling of a long, continuous arbor. A pergola is normally a more substantial structure that runs for several feet (meters) or may be quite long indeed.

OPPOSITE TOP: At Newton Vineyard in St. Helena, California, two tiers of rose pergolas give way to a majestic view.

OPPOSITE BOTTOM: Young scarlet runner beans (in bloom) will soon cover a simple pergola.

LEFT: A rustic pergola with a strong "Y" showcases a variety of roses—'Wedding Day', 'Bleu Magenta', and 'Botany Bay'.

Whatever its size, an arbor or pergola becomes a focal point in the garden. The color of the arbor or pergola may set it off, or blend it into the background, thus allowing the plant material to be the focus. If painted white, the structure becomes visually important; painted green or brown, it will present the illusion that the plants are climbing up on their own. If you are using lighting in your garden, you can have fun with an arbor or a pergola. For dramatic effect, both lend themselves to uplighting, accenting the plants climbing up the sides. Try crosslighting the top area, pointing lights across the top from either side.

GAZEBOS

A gazebo should probably be a minimum of ten feet (3m) in diameter; anything smaller will likely be too crowded for entertaining, better suited as an intimate space for one or two. In areas where mosquitoes and other night pests are a problem, consider having the gazebo screened in, or have roll-up mosquito netting to cover the openings. Before buying or building a gazebo, consider your entertaining needs. Do you want to use the gazebo as a vantage point for solo bird-watching, for dinners for two, or for cocktail parties for a dozen or more? Be sure to allow enough space for seating and any other furniture you might wish. Standing for any length of time in a gazebo can make you quickly forget the charm of the space and wish for a comfortable seat.

Gazebos are often painted white. Most people want a structure like this, one that is a major capital investment, to be highly visible. You can uplight the gazebo, either from a distance or up close, so you can enjoy the picture it makes in the landscape at night. Be sure to view the lighting from within the gazebo before it is permanently installed, though. What

TOP: Gazebos can be constructed from a variety of different materials. This octagonal wooden gazebo is ready for planting; with the right selection of vines, this structure could look verdant in relatively little time.

BOTTOM: This classic temple with stone supports and wrought iron work provides an anchor for red roses.

OPPOSITE: Two metal arches intersect to form this airy gazebo adorned with variegated ivies climbing the legs.

might look beautiful from a distant vantage point could create a tremendous glare for occupants of the gazebo.

Take special care when choosing the plantings that will surround and climb the gazebo. Most people find that the only time they have to really enjoy a gazebo is at night, so it is especially effective to include a night-blooming vine such as moonflower for its majestic blossoms and heavenly fragrance. Don't include more than a few fragrant plants, however, because the combined scents can become overwhelming and clash with each other. Your eyes drift heavenward as you sit in gazebo, so be sure to site it so that you get a view of the night sky in at least one direction. Sit quietly and you will probably see some night pollinators and nocturnal animals wandering around the garden.

Be sure to check with your local authorities before putting up any permanent structure such as a gazebo on your property. You may need a building permit. It is better to submit to local ordinances regarding construction rather than risk having the authorities tear down a structure that they have not approved or that is not built to code. (Yes, they can do that!)

CAGES

In Pennsylvania I saw what looked like a twenty-foot (6m) metal bird cage. It turned out to be an old corn crib that had been put to a new use, with hardy kiwi climbing up and over it. What a delight to walk inside the cage, and pick the ripe, large grape–size fruits and pop them into my mouth. Cages can be of a more practical size, used to surround tomato plants or support a rambling rose. They may be strictly utilitarian or, in the case of some of the English and French *tuteurs* (plant cages), so ornamental that people place them in the garden as art objects by themselves.

You can weave a rustic tepee from reeds or other vines. This tepee was constructed so that it would be narrow enough on the bottom to fit into the container, yet tall enough to allow sweet peas to twine up.

A-FRAMES, STAKES, AND TEPEES

These are the simplest of the supports, most often handmade. A single plastic stake or green-painted bamboo pole, however, is inexpensively purchased at the local garden center. Either works well to allow a single vine to climb. Twining vines can wend their way upward easily, but scramblers such as tomatoes need to be attached to the stake. To do this, wrap the tie loosely around the plant and then wind it around and tie it to the stake, forming a figure eight. Allow some leeway for the stem to grow and expand without constriction. You can buy different types of ties, from twist-ties to plastic ties. (Don't use ties with wire in the center as they are likley to damage the stem). Recycle household materials—tear up old shirts or shorts for colorful ties if you like. One gardener went so far as to use her ex-husband's ties to attach her tomato vines to stakes. Old nylon stockings and panty hose are excellent material, with enough stretch to keep the plant loosely bound. They also make a good sling to support a melon, large gourd, or cucumber that is growing from an upwardly mobile vine. Be sure to tie both ends of the sling to the support; netting may provide enough support, but chicken or turkey wire (though more unseemly) works better.

Create an A-frame of any height or length using wood, PVC pipe, or plastic stakes. Use wood, netting, or twine for cross support. Let your imagination run wild. Put six or eight stakes in a circle, lash the tops together, and you have created an instant tepee. Every child loves to have her own hidey-hole in the garden, and a tepee with scarlet runner beans and 'Jack Be Little' pumpkins running up the stakes is a perfect place to play, with scarlet red (edible) flowers, delicious beans, and tiny jack-o'-lanterns all over the outside.

VINES WITH TENDRILS		ZONES
Porcelain Berry	*Ampelopsis brevipedunculata*	5–8
Coral Vine	*Antigonon leptopus*	8–10
Cross Vine	*Bignonia capreolata*	7–10
Clematis	*Clematis* spp.	4–10
Violet Trumpet Vine	*Clytostoma callistegioides*	9–10
Trumpet Vine	*Distictis* spp.	9–10
Boston Ivy	*Parthenocissus tricuspidata*	4–10
Virginia Creeper	*Parthenocissus quinquefolia*	4–10
Passionflower	*Passiflora* spp.	9–10
Grape	*Vitis* spp.	6–10
Cape Grape	*Rhiocissus capensis*	10
Cape Honeysuckle	*Tecomaria capensis*	9–10
Orange Clockvine	*Thunbergia gibsonii*	Annual
Star Jasmine	*Trachelospermum jasminoides*	8–10
Grape	*Vitis* spp.	6–10
Wisteria	*Wisteria* spp.	5–9

LIVING SUPPORTS

In her book *Sunflower Houses*, Sharon Lovejoy describes a more elaborate child's hideaway. Sunflowers are planted to form a square or rectangle, and then morning glory seeds are sown at the base of each sunflower. Twine is strung across the tops of the sunflowers. When it is fully grown, the sunflower house has a sky-blue morning-glory roof.

Certainly the most frugal, environmentally aware way to provide support for vines and climbers is to let them grow up another plant (providing this doesn't harm the support plant). It can also be very imaginative. Bob Titus, who has a marvelous rose garden on Long Island, uses nontraditional supports for some of his climbing and rambling roses. A very hardy rose with lovely yellow flowers, 'Elegans', grows up and through a dogwood tree into a blue cedar—what an unusual and lovely sight to behold.

After a very severe winter on the East Coast in 1993–1994, many gardeners found that some of their trees and shrubs did not survive. Experts cautioned against removing seemingly dead plants before the end of the growing season, as there might be enough life left in the roots to stimulate some growth. Most gardeners ignored the advice, but in Orwigsburg, Pennsylvania, Barbara Pressler took it to heart. The thorny branches of her hardy oranges did not revive, but they did become a unique vision with morning glories and moonflowers twining around them, blooming their hearts out. Several years later, she still has the "skeleton trees" as she calls them, as support for her ever-changing cast of climbers.

In southern California, palm trees are the supports for clambering night-blooming cactus, going up forty feet (12.2m) or more. I grow the same cactus on my Long Island windowsill. Puny as they are with all my care, I dream of seeing them in their native habitat the one night of the year that they are in bloom. In the dream, the entire trunk of the palm tree comes to life as the ten-inch (25.4cm) flowers open one by one, perfuming the entire garden. I content myself with the reality of my climate, however, and was rewarded one night when my cactus flowers bloomed indoors. So despite not having all my vines and climbers on their native living supports, I can enjoy the moonflowers that encircle the sunroom windows in late summer, the cypress vine and *Mina*

At Minnesota Landscape Arboretum, Oriental bittersweet (*Celastrus orbiculatus*) is allowed to climb this fence, isolated from other areas where it could spread. The birdhouse at the base provides shelter, while the vine provides the birds with food.

A cherry tree is a handsome foil for *Hedera helix* 'Buttercup'. The thriving mosses indicate that the cool moist conditions that ivy also loves prevail in this setting.

lobata that twine along the wood fence that hides my garden tools and pots, and the spectacle of my cactus in bloom (even though it was only two flowers).

The bottom line is that, whether living or non-living, the supporting players in any garden add to its beauty and splendor. A gazebo, resplendent with morning glories and fragrant moonflowers climbing up its posts, is a magical place from which to enjoy the rest of the garden. A pergola provides cooling shade in summer, while supporting even strong climbers such as wisteria, grape, or hydrangea. Add a romantic touch with a rose arbor. Even a simple picket fence is softened and transformed with fragrant sweet peas twining among the uprights.

DECIDUOUS VINES		ZONES
Kiwi	*Actinidia* spp.	8–10
Trumpet Creeper	*Campsis* spp.	4–8
Bittersweet	*Celastrus* spp.	3–9
Clematis	*Clematis* spp.	4–10
Climbing Hydrangea	*Hydrangea anomala* ssp. *petiolaris*	5–9
Boston Ivy	*Parthenocissus tricuspidata*	4–10
Virginia Creeper	*Parthenocissus quinquefolia*	4–10
Passionflower	*Passiflora* spp.	9–10
Silver Lace Vine	*Polygonum aubertii*	5–10
Climbing Rose	*Rosa* hybrids	5–10
Grape	*Vitis* spp.	6–10
Wisteria	*Wisteria* spp.	5–9

CHAPTER
3

Growing Up

Gardening is good exercise, especially the lifting and stretching involved in working with vines and climbers. Raising your own plants from seed is a lot of fun and can save you a good deal of money. You are also likely (especially with vegetables) to find a greater variety of seeds than young plants at a nursery. Take tomatoes, for example. Consider that the average packet of seeds costs less than two dollars. That packet can provide you with up to fifty or more plants (more than enough plants to share with friends, neighbors, and relatives), each of which will yield ten pounds (4.5kg) or more of tomatoes. If tomatoes sell for a minimum of sixty-nine cents a pound (at the height of the season) at the market, then even if you grow only three or four plants, you are far ahead of the game, economically speaking. If that isn't persuasive enough, taste those supermarket tomatoes and then try a home-grown tomato—there is no comparison. The flavor alone is worth it.

For years gardeners were exhorted to grow vegetables in large, fenced-in gardens, with plants grown in neat rows. Each spring they were encouraged to till the entire bed and then plant it. Crop rotation was suggested to keep the soil in one area from becoming depleted of certain nutrients. Initially the best way to prepare the bed was to double-dig it, a technique that involves a lot of back-breaking labor, digging down twenty-four inches (61cm) and completely turning all the soil.

Today, gardeners look to less labor-intensive methods. Studies have found that continual tilling of the soil does not improve it. In fact, tilling brings weed seeds, which may be far enough below the soil surface to remain dormant, up to a level where they will sprout, making more weeding necessary. The latest research shows that, in soil that is *not* mulched, the top one-quarter to one-half inch (6–12mm) of the soil is virtually dead and contains none of the myriad microorganisms. The top layer is, in effect, sterilized by the sun. When you till, you mix the "dead" soil down into the fertile area, and bring fertile soil to the top where sunlight will eventually kill it. It seems much more logical to leave well enough alone, and to add mulch to protect the upper layer of soil.

SOIL, LIVING DIRT

Big, strong, healthy (and in the case of edibles, delicious) plants grow from healthy soil. Soil is not just dirt. It is a living substance in which diverse biological, chemical, and physical forces are constantly at work. Soil is not a single substance; it can be broken down into five major components: air (oxygen, nitrogen, and so forth), living organisms (from microscopic bacteria, viruses, and fungi to earthworms and insects), humus (organic matter in varying states of decay), water, and inorganic matter (minerals and rock particles).

For each plant in the A to Z of Plants (Chapter 4), information is provided on cultivation, describing the best conditions for growing that particular plant. Before planting your garden, become familiar with your soil. There are different types of soil, and to grow the best plants you need to know what the soil type is in the spot you wish to plant. The soil in any area may vary greatly. This is a function of how it was used and treated in the past. An area that once had been used as a path would have very compacted soil. A former garden would have a rich, loose loam. Beware of areas close to the house, especially if the house has old paint on it. The soil may be contaminated with lead from the paint, and you do not want to plant edibles in such an area. In fact, it is best to remove that soil and have it taken away by a professional licensed to dispose properly of contaminated soil.

PAGE 34: At the Children's Garden at Longwood Gardens in Pennsylvania, a scarecrow watches over a festive tepee planted with bottle gourds and 'Jack Be Nimble' pumpkins.

PAGE 35: Passion vine leaves are attractive even before the vine flowers.

RIGHT: As in gardening of any kind, it is important to choose the soil and location best suited to each vine. The result will be healthier, heartier plants, like this *Akebia quinata*, seen here in fruit.

TOP: Red passion vine (*Passiflora coccinea*) has lovely trilobed leaves and brilliant scarlet flowers, making it an eye-catching addition to any location.

BOTTOM: Many flowering vines attract bees as their pollinators. Here, a bee pauses in the midst of a busy day to drink from the dew caught in the flower of a cup-and-saucer vine (*Cobaea scandens*).

Soil samples can be sent to a laboratory for a complete analysis, but that can be costly. It is easy to determine the basic type of soil you have without much fuss or bother. Gently squeeze a small amount of moist soil in the palm of your hand, then rub it between your fingers. Sandy soil will feel gritty. Of all soil types, sandy soil is made up of the largest particles. It will not hold together when squeezed. Sandy soil is easy to dig in. It drains well, but for many plants, it drains too quickly and nutrients do not remain long enough in the root zone to be of benefit. Silt feels smooth. It can be squeezed, but it does not stay compacted, especially when it is dry. Clay, or heavy soil, is made of the smallest particles. It holds its shape when compressed, and feels slick when rubbed between the fingers. Uncompressed, clay can absorb and hold a large amount of water; the disadvantage is that it does not allow for air and water movement, which is important for plants. The ideal garden soil is loam. Loam is a mixture of sand, silt, and clay. When rubbed between the fingers it easily breaks up. It holds moisture well, while allowing for good drainage. It has the attributes to support all the biological activity necessary for a healthy garden.

The major source of food and water for a plant is the soil, so it pays to create the best soil possible. Ideally, your soil should have plenty of organic matter, good drainage, and an abundance of nutrients available to plants. Any and all soils can benefit from the addition of organic matter. When creating a new bed, turn the soil with a pitchfork or spade, and break up any large clods. Add at least ten to fifteen pounds (4.5–6.8kg) of compost or well-rotted manure, two pounds (0.9kg) of rock phosphate, and two pounds (0.9kg) of granite meal per hundred square feet (93 sq m). Whenever you are planting an existing bed, amend the soil in each planting hole as you plant with several of handfuls of compost, half a cup (125ml) of rock phosphate, and half a cup of granite meal.

pH DEMYSTIFIED

Many gardeners do not know about or understand exactly what soil pH is. A measurement of alkalinity and acidity, pH ranges on a scale from 0 (most acid) to 14 (most alkaline), with 7 as neutral. If the soil pH does not meet the requirement for a particular plant, the plant is unable to get the nutrients it needs from the soil. There are simple home kits for pH testing. County Cooperative Extension offices offer pH testing for a nominal fee, as do some nurseries and garden centers. Be sure to check the pH in several locations, as it can vary greatly from one spot to another on your property.

Once you determine the pH of the soil, and have looked up the pH requirement of the plants you want, you will know whether you need to alter the pH of the soil to suit the plants. It is a good idea to plan a garden so that plants with the same pH preferences grow in the same area. Keep acid-loving plants together, away from areas where you might add lime (such as the lawn). To lower the pH and make the soil more acid (less alkaline), add elemental sulfur (applied according to package directions). Add pelletized dolomitic limestone (again, follow package directions) to raise the pH, "sweetening" the soil, making it more alkaline (less acid).

MULCH: DRESSING THE SOIL

One of the most important things you can do for any garden is mulch. Mulching with organic material is a great time- and money-saver. A layer of several inches of organic mulch benefits the garden in many ways. Most importantly it cuts down on weeds, which in turn cuts down on the time and energy you have to spend weeding the garden. It helps to conserve water, reducing moisture loss from the soil through evaporation. Another benefit of mulch is that it keeps the soil temperature relatively stable. Eventually an organic mulch will break down, adding humus to the soil, improving the soil structure, and providing nutrients. For optimum benefit from mulch, add several inches when planting, then add more in the middle of the growing season, because the lower layer of mulch decays and becomes part of the soil. You need several inches of mulch to prevent weed seeds in the upper layers of soil from germinating. Mulch well early in the season so there will not be an inch (2.5cm) of bare soil for weeds to take root. In areas of the country without frost, winter is the ideal time to mulch the garden.

There are numerous organic mulches from which to choose. Although some are available only regionally, there should be several to fit your needs. Some mulches may be free, while others can be a bit pricey (but may be worth it for their attractiveness in a small area, or a large area if money is no object). Choose the mulch you prefer—formal or natural looking—from the following: grass clippings, straw, cocoa hulls, peanut hulls, pecan hulls, buckwheat hulls, pine needles, wood chips, wood shavings, sawdust, shredded bark, pine bark nuggets, chopped oak or other leaves, well-rotted manure, or ground corncobs. Add some nitrogen-rich organic fertilizer to the soil when mulching to keep the carbon-nitrogen ratio of the soil in balance.

LET IT ROT: COMPOST

Don't be put off by the purported complexity of composting. Composting can be as simple or as elaborate as you wish. The simplest way to compost is to have two bins. They need not be fancy; rabbit wire or fencing can be shaped into a thirty-six-inch-square (91.5 × 91.5cm) bin. Leave one side com-

Coarse bark mulch gives a clean yet rustic look atop the soil.

pletely open, or hinge a side for easier access. Start out with a couple of inches of soil (the good stuff with all those worms and microorganisms). Add small garden weeds and cuttings, any material less than a half-inch (12mm) in diameter; larger pieces take too long to break down. (Make a brush pile for larger things.) Add shredded leaves (run them over with the lawnmower), grass clippings (a layer no thicker than one inch [2.5cm] as they compact), and kitchen garbage except animal products. Vegetable peels, leftover cooked vegetables, coffee grounds, eggshells (the exception to the animal rule), and moldy lettuce left in the crisper, are all perfect for the compost pile. When you compost, you eliminate any guilt about throwing out unused food. It all goes back to nourish the earth, which will provide you with next year's food and flowers. Sprinkle in a handful of lime. Lightly water the pile to start, and then water the pile every week or two only if it doesn't rain or snow. Keep adding to the pile as you accumulate compostable material. The reason for having two bins is that when one is filled, you can start the second. Usually by the time the second bin is filled, the material in the first has broken down into compost, or "black gold." No turning, no muss, no fuss.

FERTILIZERS: NUMBERS AND LETTERS

Most gardeners are as confused about the three numbers on packages of fertilizer as they are about what pH means. Now that you understand pH, it is time to explain about fertilizers. Those three numbers (such as "5-10-5") represent the percentage of the elements nitrogen, phosphorus, and potassium in the fertilizer. This is called the N-P-K ratio (the letters are the respective chemical symbols for the elements). Each of the three elements affects a plant in a specific way. Nitrogen promotes leaf growth. Phosphorus promotes strong roots, speeds up maturity, and is essential for seed and fruit development. Potassium, also called potash, is necessary for cell division in roots and buds.

There are several organic choices for fertilizers. Nitrogen is readily available in blood meal, cottonseed meal, fish meal, and fish emulsion. Activated sewage sludge is also a good source of nitrogen, but it may be high in heavy metals, so do not use it on any edibles. Phosphorus is contained in bone meal and rock phosphate. The best sources for potassium are granite dust, ash from hardwoods, and banana skins (dug in).

THE WATER OF LIFE

Plants cannot exist without water. If you are in a drought area and are at times prohibited from watering your garden, it would be foolhardy to plant vining vegetables or annuals. Because they grow for one season only, they do not have sufficient time to develop a deep root system that could tolerate a drought. In general, vining vegetables and annuals need TLC—specifically, the nurturing, attention, and water necessary to develop properly and put on such extraordinary growth in a short time.

Since you have to water the garden, it makes sense to make the best use of what water you have. The most efficient method to use is drip irrigation. In such a system, water is released at ground level, right above where the roots are. Only minimal water loss occurs through evaporation. Because the leaves of the plants are kept dry, fungal diseases can often be avoided. A variety of do-it-yourself kits are available at nurseries, garden centers, and by mail order. You can easily create a system customized for your garden's needs, complete with emitters, supply lines, and timers. An alternative is to snake

Creating a good garden takes work. Make it easy on yourself and use a wheelbarrow (or two) or a garden cart for hauling soil, amendments, and plants. Keep honeysuckle pruned to keep it from growing out of control. In contrast, Clematis and *Hedera helix* 'Goldheart' are well behaved and rarely require pruning. Once you've planted, it will be no time before the vines and climbers are growing up and out, adding color and beauty to your garden.

"leaky pipe" hoses through the garden. These are made of recycled tires, through which water can slowly seep, again delivering water at ground level, near the root zone. Using either of these methods, you can water the plants at any time of day or night. If you use a traditional sprinkler or above-ground watering system, however, water early in the morning so the leaves have time to dry off before they receive full sun.

SUN AND SHADE

Like the need for soil and water, the need for light is fundamental to all plants. All green plants need light to grow, because sunlight is essential for the process of photosynthesis. Plants will not grow in complete darkness; all you can grow under those conditions are mushrooms. Each plant has a preference for a type of light, ranging from full sun to partial shade. "Full sun" is defined as more than six hours of direct, unfiltered sunlight a day, including at least two hours at the peak time when the sun is directly overhead, from 10 A.M. to 2 P.M. "Shade" is often divided into three types: light shade, partial shade, and full shade. Plants in light shade get six hours of near-full sun a day, or lightly dappled shade throughout the sunlight hours. In warm climates, light shade can be better for plants than full sun. In the heat of the day, plants in light shade are less likely to dry out, get scorched, or sunburned. Light shade gives you the widest range of plant material to choose from, including most sun-loving plants and many plants that are partial to more shade. Partial, medium, or half shade indicates less sun, usually four to six hours a day, or a heavier dappled shade throughout the day. Full shade offers no more than four hours of sun a day, or heavily dappled sunlight all day. Thus it is not a matter of simple black and white, sun or no sun.

VINES FOR SHADE		ZONES
Kiwi	*Actinidia* spp.	8–10
Five-Leaf Akebia	*Akebia quinata*	4–10
Dutchman's Pipe	*Aristolochia durior*	4–1
Bittersweet	*Celastrus* spp.	3–9
Clematis	*Clematis* spp.	4–10
Violet Trumpet Vine	*Clytostoma callistegioides*	9–10
Trumpet Vine	*Distictis* spp.	9–10
Winter Creeper	*Euonymus fortunei*	4–8
Fatshedera	× *Fatshedera lizei*	9–10
Creeping Fig	*Ficus pumila*	9–10
Yellow Jessamine	*Gelsemium sempervirens*	7–10
English Ivy	*Hedera helix*	5–10
Gold Guinea Plant	*Hibbertia scandens*	10
Climbing Hydrangea	*Hydrangea anomala* ssp. *petiolaris*	5–9
Jasmine	*Jasminum* spp.	8–10
Honeysuckle	*Lonicera* spp.	4–10
Moonseed	*Menispermum canadense*	3–10
Boston Ivy	*Parthenocissus tricuspidata*	4–10
Virginia Creeper	*Parthenocissus quinquefolia*	4–10
Silver Lace Vine	*Polygonum aubertii*	5-10
Cape Grape	*Rhiocissus capensis*	10
Cape Honeysuckle	*Tecomaria capensis*	9–1
Orange Clockvine	*Thunbergia gibsonii*	Annual
Star Jasmine	*Trachelospermum jasminoides*	8–10
Grape	*Vitis* spp.	6–10
Wisteria	*Wisteria* spp.	5–9

PESTS AND DISEASES

It is the rare garden that is totally pest-free. However, interplanting a wide variety of plants usually results in a healthier garden than one that is a monoculture. Studies have found that some plants seem to protect others from infestations. Conversely, some plants seem to inhibit the growth of others. Try to include in any group one or two plants that persist through the winter (a small tree or shrub, a dwarf evergreen), which may provide a safe haven for praying mantises to deposit their egg cases. Praying mantises eat a prodigious number of aphids, whiteflies, and other garden pests.

Keep a birdbath nearby to encourage birds in the garden. They may be pests of some of the small fruits, but in general birds are worth having around for the caterpillars and other insect pests that they will eat. They too will appreciate a small tree or shrub in which to perch while sizing up the garden. And something as simple as a clay pot turned on its side in a shady spot in the garden can help in the war against pests. It may attract a frog or toad, both of which love an insect lunch.

If you suspect that you have a pest or disease problem, be sure it is properly identified. Do not just go out into the garden and randomly start spraying—you will more than likely kill as many of the good bugs as the bad ones. Your county's Cooperative Extension Service can be of help; many have telephone hot lines and allow you to bring in plants and pests for identification. Hand-pick insects early in the morning, when they are slow to react. If only a small section of a plant is diseased, cut it out and get rid of that portion. Never put diseased material on the compost pile. Dip pruners in alcohol after every cut to avoid spreading disease.

Avoid using any chemical in the garden, even the so-called "organic" ones, because they still affect all the creatures that live in the garden, good and bad. It is best to try and live in harmony with your garden.

TOP: When leaves begin to brown, it's a signal to to take a closer look for possible pests or disease. Make sure plants, especially tomatoes such as this 'Super Sweet 100', are getting ample water and that the soil is the proper pH.

BOTTOM: These cucumbers show signs of calcium deficiency. The veins of the leaf remain green while the leaf yellows from the margins inward.

LEFT: Yellowing of leaves may be indicative of a nitrogen deficiency, especially with heavy feeders such as cucumbers. To combat this, foliar feed the plant with manure tea or diluted liquid kelp.

RIGHT: Placing feeders in and around the garden is an excellent way to attract pest-eating birds to your garden.

A to Z of Plants

This A-to-Z listing is actually three listings—the first covers edibles, the second covers ornamental annuals and tender perennials, and the third covers ornamental perennials and woody vines. Each list is alphabetized according to the common name and each entry is cross-referenced to related plants, where applicable. For every planting, the genus and species (that is, the botanic name) are included below the common name, followed by the family name in parentheses. Finally, a comprehensive list of alternate common names is included for every planting that has more than one common name.

The range of vines and climbers is vast. These plants run the gamut from purely ornamental evergreens such as English ivy to those grown for their exquisite flowers, such as bougainvillea. Others have several qualities that endear them to gardeners. In my opinion, plants that are edible

as well as ornamental deserve top priority in any garden. As you plan your garden, consider planting some of these delightful, delicious edibles in a place of distinction. Take them out of the traditional boundary of the vegetable patch and use them as dual-purpose landscape plants.

If a plant listed in the A to Z appeals to you, but is not within your hardiness range, you can probably still grow it. In cold winter areas, grow nonhardy plants in containers or in the ground once the weather has warmed. In autumn, before a killing frost, you can move the plant inside and keep it in a suitable location (one that is warm enough and receives ample light). In a tropical region, where the summers may be too hot to grow certain plants, you might be able to grow those plants in spring or fall, when the weather is more moderate. Whatever your climate, there are many vines and climbers to grace your garden.

EDIBLES

American Grape

Vitis labrusca (Vitaceae)

Also known as fox or Concord grapes, American grapes are native to the Northeast, grow in bunches, and are the hardiest of the grapes. They are distinguished by their skin, which easily slips off the fruit. Delicious eaten out of hand, they are well-suited for making into jellies and juice. Some American grapes: large purple 'Alden'; blue 'Beta'; widely grown, light green 'California Thompson Seedless'; the preeminent 'Concord', against which all other American grapes are judged; 'Concord Seedless'; sweet, pale red 'Delaware'; sweet, white 'Edelweiss'; early ripening 'Fredonia' black grape; great white, very hardy 'Himrod'; and 'New York Muscat', a reddish-black dessert grape. See Grape (page 57) for cultivating tips.

Apple Melon

Cucumis melo, Chito group (Cucurbitaceae)

This warty, oblong-to-oval, orange-yellow, bitter fruit (also called mango melon, vegetable orange, garden lemon, and vine peach) is used in Asian cuisine. It is best grown on a trellis. See Melon (page 63) for cultivating tips.

Asparagus Bean

Vigna unguiculata ssp. *sesquipedalis* (Fabaceae)

Asparagus bean (also known as Chinese long bean, snake bean, and dow guak) is a handsome vine with medium-green leaves and beans up to 3 feet (91.5cm) long, thus living up to its other common name, yard-long bean. The beans are best eaten when 10 to 12 inches (25.5–30.5cm) long, when the thin pods are very crunchy.

ASPARAGUS BEAN

grows 6 to 8 feet (1.8–2.4m) tall, and is hardy in Zones 7 to 10. The somewhat triangular leaves are handsome as a backdrop in the garden. Purplish-red flowers, grouped in loose clusters, give rise to distinctively four-sided, winged pods. In addition, the plant produces marble-size edible tubers that are excellent in soups, stews, and stir-fries.

This plant requires a long, hot growing season; in cold areas, it may not even flower. Allow 120 to 150 frost-free days for harvesting the pods, 180 to 210 frost-free days to harvest the tubers. Grow along a trellis or fence for support. Asparagus peas thrive in full sun in loose, well-drained soil with pH 7.3 to 8.0. Plant peas 1 inch (2.5cm) deep and 2 to 4 inches (5–10cm) apart after all danger of frost has passed. Harvest the pods when they are 6 to 8 inches (15–20.5cm) long. For best flavor, wait to dig the tubers until frost has killed back the plants.

Balsam Apple

Momordica balsamina (Cucurbitaceae)

An Oriental food plant related to the bitter melon, balsam apple is grown in North America primarily for ornamentation. The fruit grows only 3 inches (7.6cm) long, with tapered ends. The arils inside are brilliant red, giving rise to its name. See Bitter Melon (page 48) for cultivating tips.

BEAN

Phaseolus spp. (Fabaceae)

Included in this group are those varieties of beans that are eaten in their entirety (pod and all), such as string beans, and those from which the pod is removed and only the bean itself is eaten, such as lima beans. Depending on the particular variety of fresh bean, they grow anywhere from Zone 3 and warmer. Some catalogs carry varieties that are quicker to mature, suited to more northern climes.

Beans need full sun and good air circulation. Grow them in well-drained soil that is not too fertile, with pH 6.0 to 7.5. Most beans and peas perform

BEAN

Asparagus bean grows best in warm weather, requiring a minimum of seventy-five frost-free days to mature. It needs a trellis for support. See Bean (below) for cultivating tips.

Asparagus Pea

Psophocarpus tetragonolobus (Fabaceae)

The asparagus pea (also called Goa bean, winged bean, Manila bean, princess pea, and winged pea), best known in Asian cuisine, is rapidly gaining popularity in America. Native to the tropics, this perennial vine better when an innoculant (actually freeze-dried nitrogen-fixing bacteria, widely available) is added at planting time—before planting, lightly moisten the beans, remove excess moisture, toss them in a plastic bag with the innoculant, then plant. Sow beans directly in the garden after all danger of frost has passed and the soil has warmed up. Plant three or four beans 1 inch (2.5cm) apart in a cluster, with clusters spaced 2 to 3 feet (61–91.5cm) from each other. Bean seedlings are a favorite of birds, so if the seedlings seem to disappear overnight, replant and protect with row covers to keep marauders at bay. Pole beans will continue to produce beans as long as they are kept regularly picked.

Mulch well to keep soil temperature constant and to prevent moisture loss. Keep the plants well watered, especially when they are in flower. Provide some means of support for the vines, like a trellis or strong netting. Pole beans are ready to harvest about ten weeks after planting, and runner beans after about thirteen weeks. Dry beans can be harvested about six weeks after the blossoms first appear. See also Asparagus Bean (page 46), Lima Bean (page 62), Pole Bean (page 66), and Runner Bean (page 67).

Bitter Melon

Momordica charantia (Cucurbitaceae)

Used in Chinese cooking, bitter melon (also known as balsam pear, bitter cucumber, and la-kwa) is a fast-growing, tropical, perennial vine usually grown as an annual. The showy fruit ranges in size from 1 to 8 inches long (2.5–20.3cm). It grows well from Zones 7 to 11. In these areas with long warm summers, the vines bear somewhat oblong, warty fruits with pale green, waxy skin, maturing to an orange blush. The drying rind splits to show off the vivid scarlet arils that surround the seeds (white or brown).

Bitter melon requires full sun and rich, well-drained soil with pH 6.0 to 6.5. In all but the warmest areas (where you can seed directly into the garden), start the seeds in pots indoors six to eight weeks before the last frost in spring. After all danger of frost has passed and the soil is warm,

BITTER MELON

BLACKBERRY

transplant into the garden, allowing at least 24 inches (61cm) between plants. Support this prolific vine with a strong trellis, fence, wall, or arbor.

For eating, harvest the fruits when they are immature, no longer than 6 inches (15cm) in length, or they become too bitter and chewy. For ornamental purposes, allow the fruit to remain on the vine until maturity.

In the Orient, two distinct edible varieties are grown, those with long and those with short fruit. The longer variety is more readily available in North America. See also Balsam Apple (page 47) and Hercules' War Club Gourd (page 58).

Blackberry

Rubus ulmifolius (Rosaceae)

Blackberries are one of the two main types of brambleberries. They grow like raspberries, but are more tender (Zones 5 to 8). When planting, allow 4 to 6 feet (1.2–1.8m) between trailing types; 'Thornless Evergreen' is especially vigorous, so allow 10 feet (3m) between plants. Recommended varieties include easy-picking 'Bristol'; long-season 'Darrow'; early, purplish 'Ebony King'; flavorful 'Illini'; and nonsuckering 'Thornfree'.

Boysenberry

Rubus ursinus 'Boysen' (Rosaceae)

Drought-resistant, boysenberries have distinctively flavored fruit that look like large, elongated raspberries, dark red ripening to purplish-black. A single plant can yield ten pounds (4.5kg) of fruit. Allow 8 feet (2.4m) between plants. Boysenberries, the most tender of the trailing blackberries, grow in Zones 8 and 9. Shiny black 'Olallie' grows best in California. See Brambleberry (below) for cultivating tips.

BRAMBLEBERRY

Rubus spp. (Rosaceae)

The brambleberries include black raspberry, boysenberry, red raspberry, thornless blackberry, and hybrids. They are all deciduous, bushy plants with biennial canes, growing from 5 to 26 feet (1.5–8m) tall, depending on the species. Most canes are prickly to thorny; some thornless varieties are available. Berries are delicious picked fresh from the plant and popped into your mouth, put on morning cereal, or made into jam, pie, or even wine.

Trained on wires or a trellis, brambleberries make an excellent impenetrable hedge. Kept well pruned, these bushes can be an attractive addition to the landscape. Most have dark green leaves that are lighter on the underside, and white flowers in clusters followed by red or black berries (there are a few varieties with white or yellow fruit).

Brambleberries are usually divided into two major types: raspberries and blackberries. Raspberry-type berries easily come off the plant with no core, while blackberries come with a core.

Brambleberries need full sun; in areas with hot summers they prefer partial shade. Grow them in well-drained soil amended with lots of organic material (well-rotted manure or compost). Mulch well around the plants with compost or leaves. Fertilize judiciously in spring with manure. Overfertilizing will result in lots of growth but few berries. Keep the plants lightly moist; do not let them dry out.

Brambleberries are best controlled when trained (tied) to a fence or wire. Pruning methods vary with type. Single crop fruit— those that bear once, on second-year wood—can be pruned to the ground after the fruit is harvested. Tie five or six of the new canes to the wire; these will fruit the following year. Everbearing red raspberries bear fruit in fall and again the following spring. After fall harvest, cut back the tops of the fruiting canes. The lower branches will fruit in spring. After spring fruiting, cut the canes down completely.

Brambleberries are best picked when they are fully colored and sweet. Keep picking berries every couple of days. They bruise easily, so handle with care. Trailing varieties generally yield one quart of berries per foot (30.5cm) of row; erect, shrubby types yield about one quart per 2 feet (61cm) of row. See also Blackberry (page 49), Boysenberry (page 49), Dewberry (page 54), Japanese Wineberry (page 60), Loganberry (page 62), Marionberry (page 63), Raspberry (page 67), Sunberry (page 70), Tayberry (page 71), and Tummelberry (page 73).

Buttercup Squash

Cucurbita maxima (Cucurbitaceae)

A good winter-keeper squash, buttercup has dark green, blocky fruit with a turban at one end. Buttercup matures in 105 days. See Squash (page 68) for cultivating tips.

Butternut Squash

Cucurbita moschata (Cucurbitaceae)

A good winter-keeper squash, butternut has beige to tan skin with orange flesh, a long thick neck, and a rounded base. Varieties are 'Butter Boy Hybrid' and 'Waltham Butternut'. See Squash (page 68) for cultivating tips.

BUTTERCUP SQUASH

Cantaloupe

Cucumis melo, Cantalupensis group (Cucurbitaceae)

This is the true cantaloupe, grown mostly in Europe. It does not have netted rinds of the muskmelon, which is incorrectly called cantaloupe in North America. Choice varieties include 'Charentais', 'Haogen', and 'Jivaro'. See Melon (page 63) for cultivating tips.

Casaba Melon

Cucumis melo, Inodorus group (Cucurbitaceae)

The casaba is a large, football-shaped melon with golden skin and white flesh. See Melon (page 63) for cultivating tips.

Chayote

Sechium edule (Cucurbitaceae)

Chayote (also called mirliton, cho-cho, vegetable pear, christophene, and chuchu) is a warm-climate (Zones 7 to 11), semihardy, perennial vine with edible shoots, roots, and fruits, native to tropical America. It grows to 15 feet (4.6m) long in the mid-South and up to 30 feet (9m) in the Southwest, requiring 80 to 90 frost-free days for the pear-shaped, waxy green fruits to set. The roots and shoots are not harvested until the second year.

Chayote requires full sun (at least twelve hours of sun a day to begin to set fruit) and a strong trellis, wall, or fence on which to climb. It prefers moist, well-drained soil that is deeply cultivated and fertile, with a pH between 5.5 and 6.5. In completely frost-free areas, plant directly in the garden. In all other areas, in midspring, plant two or three fruits in a one-gallon (4.5L) container. Place the fruit on its side, covering halfway with soil. Lightly moisten the soil and cover the pot with plastic wrap and put in a warm place with temperatures from 75 to 80 degrees F (23.8–26.7 °C). Water as needed. Once the seed (at the

CHAYOTE

puckered end of the fruit) has sent out a shoot, remove the plastic and set the pot in full sun in a warm place. After all danger of frost has passed and the soil has warmed, transplant into the garden, allowing 4 feet (1.2m) between plants. Water deeply at least once a week with manure tea or soluble fertilizer. Continue to feed until the first flower appears.

Harvest the immature fruit when it reaches 4 to 6 inches (10–15cm) in length and use it like summer squash. The flavor is somewhat bland; it benefits from the addition of other vegetables, herbs, and spices in cooking. The fruit is mature when it stops growing; then use it like winter squash. Harvest all fruit before frost. Refrigerate and store in a ventilated plastic bag with several paper towels (to soak up excess moisture) up to ninety days. Save several to plant the next spring. After frost, cut the entire plant back and mulch the roots. The next spring, cut the shoots to use like asparagus. The following fall, dig the roots to use (and store) like potatoes. The roots are delicious boiled, candied, or roasted.

In North America, we are limited to whatever varieties are in the market. In Central America and Mexico, a variety of chayotes are available: white, brownish, or apple-green, with skin smooth or spiny.

Crenshaw Melon

Cucumis melo, Inodorus group (Cucurbitaceae)

With its pale tan skin and delicately flavored salmon flesh, the Crenshaw melon is a favorite. Choice varieties include 'Honeyshaw' and 'Burpee Early Hybrid'. See Melon (page 63) for cultivating tips.

Cucumber

Cucumis sativus (Cucurbitaceae)

Cucumbers are annual vines with tri-lobed, pointed, rough, dark green leaves. Grown from Zone 4 south, they require 48 to 70 frost-free days to mature. There are three classes of cucumbers: pickling cucumbers

CRENSHAW MELON

CUCUMBER

(short, blocky fruits), slicing cucumbers (long, cylindrical fruits used fresh), Oriental or "burpless" cucumbers (very long, ridged fruits that supposedly do not cause repeating).

All cucumbers require full sun and good air circulation to avoid fungus and mildew. They prefer light soil amended with organic material, with pH 6.0 to 7.0. Sow seeds directly in the garden after all danger of frost has passed and the soil has warmed (about three to four weeks after the last frost date in spring). For a jump-start on the season, start seeds indoors in peat pots about four weeks before planting time. When the first true leaves appear, transplant into the garden, pot and all. Allow 12 to 15 inches (30.5 to 38cm) between plants in rows or hills of four to five plants spaced four feet apart. Mulch well and fertilize once a month. Water regularly throughout the growing season.

Cucumber vines can ramble along the ground. A space-saving trick, which also results in longer, straighter fruit, is to train them up a trellis or in a cage. For best flavor and consistency, pick the fruit when it is small: pickling cucumbers at 3 to 4 inches (7.5–10cm) long, and slicers at 6 to 8 inches (15–20.5cm). If the blossom end of the cucumber gets a yellowish tinge, it is overripe. Keep picking the cucumbers and the plant will continue to flower and fruit.

Here are some choice varieties. Slicing cucumbers: All-American winner 'Straight Eight'; Middle Eastern delicacy 'Kidma'; heirloom 'Lemon' (round and yellow); European white 'De Bouenil'; and disease-resistant 'Burpee Hybrid II'. Pickling cucumbers (cornichons, Kirby cucumbers, or gherkins) are short, crisp, and have a relatively small seed area. Try the compact and prolific 'Little Leaf'; 'Picklebush', with a 24-inch (61cm) vine; gynoecious 'Pickalot'; disease-resistant, All-American winner 'Saladin'. Oriental cucumbers include the twelve-inch (30.5cm) 'Palace King', which produces over a long season. Burpless varieties: 8-inch (20.5cm) 'Green Knight'; 10-inch (25.5cm) 'Tasty Green' (formerly 'Burpless'); 14-inch (35.5cm), virtually seedless, All-America winner 'Sweet Success'; 15- to 18-inch (38–46cm) British heirloom 'Rollinison's Telegraph'; and 15- to 18-inch (38–46cm) 'Early Perfection' (Japanese 'Bitter Free').

EDIBLE PODDED PEAS

Armenian, or "yard-long," cucumbers have a distinctive creamy, pale green color and long, smooth, deeply ridged fruit. With their perfectly scalloped edges, they are especially decorative when sliced. Two varieties are 'The Duke' and 'Armenian', growing to 2 feet (61cm) long and 2½ inches (6.5cm) in diameter.

Delicate Squash

Cucurbita pepo (Cucurbitaceae)

The oblong, green-and-ivory striped fruit of this winter-type squash (also called sweet potato squash) has orange flesh and weighs up to 2 pounds (1kg). It does not need curing. 'Delicata' and 'Sugarbush' are excellent choices. See Squash (page 68) for cultivating tips.

Dewberry

Rubus caesius (Rosaceae)

The dewberry plant, with its flavorful, blackberrylike, small berries, can be allowed to sprawl and grow as a ground cover. See Brambleberry (page 49) for cultivating tips.

Edible Podded Peas

Pisum sativum var. *macrocarpon* (Fabaceae)

This group encompasses both snow peas (sugar peas, China peas) and snap peas (sugar snap peas). The entire pod can be eaten in these varieties. Most need to be stringed before eating. Choice snow peas: 'Nori', 20 inches (51cm) tall; 'Oregon Sugar Pod II', 36 inches (91.5cm) tall; 'Snowbird', 18 inches (46cm) tall, needs no support; Burpee's 'Sweetpod Brand', 48 inches (1.2m) tall; 'Blizzard', 30 inches (76cm) tall; and 'Norli', 5 feet (1.5m) tall.

Choice snap peas: 'Honeypod', 18 inches (46cm) tall; 'Sugar Ann', 18 to 30 inches (46 to 76cm) tall; 'Sugar Gem', 26 inches (66cm) tall, stringless; 'Sugar Snap', 5 to 6 feet (1.5 to 1.8m) tall; 'Bush Snapper', 25 inches

GIANT PUMPKINS

(63.5cm) tall; 'Snappy', 6 feet (1.8m) tall; 'Sugar Bon', 24 inches (61cm) tall; 'Sugar Daddy', 30 inches (76cm) tall, stringless; 'Super Sugar Mel', 3 feet (91.5cm) tall; and 'Sugar Pop', 18 inches (46cm) tall, stringless. See Pea (page 64) for cultivating tips.

European Grape

Vitis vinifera (Vitaceae)

European grapes have tight skins and winy flavor. There are three distinct types: wine grapes, dessert grapes, and raisin grapes. They are less hardy than their American cousins, tolerating cold to only 5 degrees F (-15C). They need a good deal of summer heat to ripen sweetly. Some choice European grapes: reddish-black seedless 'Black Monukka' (both a table grape and used for raisins); the red wine grape 'Cabarnet Sauvignon'; the white wine grape 'French Columbard'; red wine 'Grenache'; musky, sweet-flavored 'Muscat of Alexandria'; green table grape 'Olivette Blanche' ('Lady Finger'); white 'White Riesling', suitable for cool areas; and red wine 'Zinfandel', which makes a good jelly. See Grape (page 57) for cultivating tips.

Giant Pumpkin

Cucurbita maxima (Cucurbitaceae)

To achieve prize-winning size, remove all but one pumpkin from the vine. 'Atlantic Giant' can reach 400 pounds (182kg); thick-fleshed 'Big Max', 100 pounds (45kg); reddish-orange, slightly flattened 'Rouge Vif d'Etampes', 30-plus pounds (14kg); 'Prizewinner Hybrid', 100-plus pounds (45kg); 'Big Moon', 200-plus pounds (91kg). See Pumpkin (page 66) for cultivating tips.

Gourd

Lagenaria siceraria (Cucurbitaceae)

Although gourds (also called bottle gourds, white-flowered gourds, cal-abashes, dipper gourds, sugar troughs, cucuzzis, po guas, and yugao) are commonly grown as ornaments, you can harvest the young fruit and eat it like summer squash. Fast-growing, perennial vines up to 30 feet (9m) long, gourds are typically grown as annuals. Most varieties have a hairy, sticky stem, broadly oval leaves, and showy white flowers. The fruit is quite variable, ranging from 3 to 36 inches (7.5–91.5cm) long; it may be somewhat flat or round, crooknecked, with a shape resembling a dipper, club, bottle, or dumbbell. Gourds grow best in Zones 5 to 10.

All gourds require full sun and rich, well-drained soil with pH 6.0 to 6.5. Allow for good air circulation (provide trellising or other strong support) to avoid mildew. Plant two or three seeds in hills directly in the garden after all danger of frost has passed. Allow 6 feet (1.8m) between hills when letting the plants ramble on the ground, less if training them to grow on a trellis. Keep vines well mulched and watered for larger fruits. Fertilize monthly.

Pick fruits for eating when they are less than seven days old and the skin is tender. Scrape off skin and remove ½ inch (1.2cm) from both ends. Prepare as you would summer squash. Harvest ornamental gourds just before first fall frost, leaving 2 to 3 inches (5–7.5cm) of stem. Allow the gourds to dry (they are dry when you hear seeds rattling around inside) for several weeks in a warm, dry, well-ventilated room. Bottle gourds can be made into birdhouses by drilling holes into them, waxing the outsides to preserve them, and hanging them from a tree. See also Serpent Gourd (page 68).

Granadilla

Passiflora quadrangularis (Passifloraceae)

Granadilla is one of the main commercial varieties of passionfruit. A strong semitropical vine, it produces fragrant, large white flowers marked with red and purple, and large yellowish-green fruits that grow to 9 inches (22.5cm) in length. See Passionfruit (page 64) for cultivating tips.

GOURD

GRAPE

GRAPE

Vitis spp. (Vitaceae)

Grapes are deciduous, woody, climbing vines that can reach from 50 to 100 feet (15–30m) in length. However, they are usually pruned to 12 to 20 feet (4.6–6m).

Not only are the fruit of grapes edible, so are the leaves. Soaked in brine, they are the wrapper for the Middle Eastern dish stuffed grape leaves (*dolmas*). The leaves are large, medium green to blue-green, and palmately lobed.

All grapes need full sun and deeply cultivated, well-drained soil. Although they are not terribly fussy about soil conditions, they will be more prolific on fertile soil. In very cold areas, consider growing grapes against a south wall; this provides shelter in the cold months and extra warmth in the summer. Use compost or well-rotted manure as a fertilizer. A sign of nitrogen deficiency is pale foliage; apply a nitrogen fertilizer before midsummer. Grapes benefit from occasional deep waterings, encouraging deep root growth. To discourage fungal diseases, water at the soil level, not from above. Discontinue watering after August to allow the plant to harden off before winter.

Train vines to climb on some sort of support. Pruning is necessary to keep them at a reasonable size and to encourage fruiting (they bear fruit on the current year's growth). Both American and wine grapes, especially when grown commercially, are often trained in the four-arm Kniffen system. The vine is pruned so that two sets of arms (upper and lower, as it were) are trained to grow laterally along two parallel wires (2 to 3 feet [61–91.5cm] between wires) supported at each end by a post. When space is not at a premium, grapes are lovely grown on an arbor or on a pergola. Where space is limited, they can be espaliered against a wall. With patience, a grape vine can be trained into the form of a small weeping tree to make a lovely garden accent.

Grapes are ready to harvest when they are fully colored and sweet-tasting. Pick the entire bunch. See also American Grape (page 46), European Grape (page 55), and Muscadine Grape (page 63).

Hercules' War Club Gourd

Lagenaria longissima (Cucurbitaceae)

Also known as upoe, the Hercules' war club gourd is a popular vegetable, especially in China. The vigorous plants produce long, thin, light green fruits that can grow to 3 feet (91.5cm) long. The fruit are best eaten when 6 inches (15cm) long; then they taste like creamy summer squash. See Bitter Melon (page 48) for cultivating tips.

Honeydew Melon

Cucumis melo, Inodorus group (Cucurbitaceae)

Honeydew has a pale green rind and flesh that is pale green to almost white. Choice varieties include 'Honey Dew', 'Venus Hybrid', 'Kazakh', and 'Honey Grow'. See Melon (page 63) for cultivating tips.

Hop

Humulus lupulus (Cannabaceae)

Hops (also called common hops, European hops, and bine) are vigorous, dioecious, tender perennial vines that can easily grow to 20 feet (6m) or more in a season. Climbing by tendrils, they quickly cover a fence, porch, pergola, or arbor. They can provide almost instant shade when trained on a trellis. Traditionally grown for the pineconelike flowers used in brewing beer, hops are more versatile in the home kitchen. Cut 6 to 8 inches (15 to 20.5cm) of the pencil-thin new shoots in spring, and cook them as you would asparagus. In creating a dish, you have also pruned the otherwise rampant vine, helping to keep it somewhat in check. If you are growing the vine for the flowers, make sure you have a female plant; males do not bear showy blooms. Other than its culinary uses, the vine can be appreciated for its purely ornamental properties. The large, fuzzy, tri-lobed leaves are a lovely light green, creating a nice background to the garden.

HOP

58

HYACINTH BEAN

Hops thrive in full sun in rich, well-drained, moist soil. They will tolerate partial shade, wind, and drought. To keep the plants in bounds, prune hard at the base of the plant each spring, removing half of the new shoots. Start training by hand, guiding the twining vines in the direction you wish. 'Aureus' has handsome yellow-green leaves.

Hubbard Squash

Cucurbita maxima (Cucurbitaceae)

A winter-type squash, hubbard has a hard rind, large, warty-looking fruit, and keeps well through winter. 'Blue Hubbard' (120 days) is the standard variety. See Squash (page 68) for cultivating tips.

Hyacinth Bean

Dolichos lablab (Fabaceae)

Hyacinth bean is frequently grown as an ornamental for its attractive wisterialike, purplish-pink blossoms and deep purple, shiny pods. It is a vining plant that grows quickly, needing support like pole beans. In warm climates it is perennial, but it may be grown as an annual elsewhere. See Bean (page 47) for cultivating tips.

Japanese Hop

Humulus japonicus (Cannabaceae)

Native to Japan, this hop is grown solely as an ornamental. An annual twining vine, it grows even faster than the European species, reaching as much

JAPANESE WINEBERRY

as 35 feet (10.5m) in a season. The hops on this plant are not very decorative, so you can grow either male or female plants. The leaves are large, 6 to 8 inches (15 to 20.5cm) wide with five to seven deeply cut lobes. Japanese hop thrives in hot weather in fertile soil in sun or shade. 'Variegatus' has handsome white-and-green variegated leaves.

Japanese Pumpkin

Cucurbita mixta (Cucurbitaceae)

Japanese pumpkins (also called Hokkaido squash or Chinese pumpkin) have green skin with sweet, moist, dark orange flesh that is good for cooking. 'Green Striped Cushaw' has a crooked neck. See Pumpkin (page 66) for cultivating tips.

Japanese Wineberry

Rubus phoenicolasius (Rosaceae)

Long arching stems covered with soft, striking red bristles make Japanese wineberry attractive in fall and winter after leaves have fallen. Golden-yellow fruit ripens to light red. Berries are small and seedy with a mild, grapelike flavor. Good for jams, jellies, and preserves. Allow 6 feet (1.8m) between plants. See Brambleberry (page 49) for cultivating tips.

Kiwi

Actinidia deliciosa (*A. chinensis*) (Actinidiaceae)

Kiwis (also known as kiwifruit and Chinese gooseberries) are vigorous, dioecious, deciduous, semihardy vines that grow to 30 feet (9m) long, requiring 235 frost-free days to produce ripe fruit. The unique, egg-shaped, fuzzy brown fruit ripens in mid- to late autumn. Peel the skin; underneath is the succulent, lime-green, translucent flesh speckled with small black seeds with a remarkable flavor of strawberry, pineapple, melon, and banana.

KIWI

The hardy kiwi (*Actinidia arguta*) has a much smaller, smooth-skinned fruit, about the size of a large grape, which can be eaten whole—no peeling necessary. The hardy kiwi is hardy to −25 degrees F (−31.7°C) and can be grown as far north as New Hampshire.

Kiwis need full sun and rich loam with excellent drainage. In the warmest areas, plant where they will get afternoon shade. As kiwis are dioecious—that is, either male or female—you need both a male and female to produce fruit. Only the female plant will bear fruit. (An exception is 'Issai', a hardy kiwi that is self-fertile.)

Vigorous growers, kiwis need the sturdy support of a trellis, arbor, pergola, fence, or wall on which to climb. Mulch thickly around the base of the vine with organic mulch. Fertilize these heavy feeders once a month during the growing season. Regular watering is essential, especially in dry regions. Do not allow the vines to dry out.

Because of their potential for growth, kiwis need to be pruned twice a year. Prune heavily when the vines are dormant to encourage fruiting. Fruiting takes place on the first three to six buds of the current year's growth. Prune the vines lightly in summer to keep them shaped and within bounds. According to some authorities, hardy kiwis may not need to be pruned.

Pick kiwis just before they begin to soften. Picked too early, they will be too tart and the fruit will shrivel. Two vines of hardy kiwi can yield ten gallons of fruit. 'Chico' and 'Hayward' are the most readily available fruiting female kiwis. 'Meader' (female or male) and 'Issai' (self-fertile) are easily found varieties of hardy kiwi.

Kuta Hybrid Squash

Cucurbita pepo (Cucurbitaceae)

Kuta hybrid squash can be picked young and used like a summer squash, or allowed to stay on the vine like a winter squash. See Squash (page 68) for cultivating tips.

Lima Bean

Phaseolus limensis var. *limenanus* (Fabaceae)

Limas are prized for their rich, flat beans that are delicious when small or dried and used (especially in winter) in soups and stews. Lima beans grow in both bush and pole varieties, with pole varieties taking longer (from eighty-five to one hundred days) to mature. Many gardeners consider the superior flavor and higher yield of pole limas worth the wait. Select varieties include 'King of the Garden Pole', 'Christmas Pole', and 'Burpee's Best', which grows to 12 feet (3.7m) tall, needing strong supports. See Bean (page 47) for cultivating tips.

Loganberry

Rubus occidentalis (Rosaceae)

The loganberry is a natural blackberry-raspberry cross with fruit larger than either parent. Its somewhat acid-flavored fruit is best cooked or frozen. This plant prefers slightly acid soil (pH about 6.0) and medium to heavy loam. See Brambleberry (page 49) for more cultivating tips.

Malabar Spinach

Basella alba (Basellaceae)

Malabar spinach (also called Ceylon spinach, Indian spinach, Malabar nightshade, pasali, and pu-tin-choi) is a vining annual whose glossy leaves can be cooked and used like spinach. Heat-loving, it grows well in warm climates where spinach is problematic (in Zone 7 and warmer), needing 120 to 150 frost-free days to mature. In optimum conditions, it can grow to 30 feet (9m); however, it is more likely to range from 6 to 10 feet (1.8–3m).

Malabar spinach requires full sun and is best trained to grow up a fence, trellis, or arbor. It prefers humusy, moist, rich soil with a pH

MALABAR SPINACH

between 6.0 and 7.5. Start the seeds indoors at least eight weeks before the last spring frost date. Transplant into the garden after all danger of frost has passed and the soil has warmed, allowing 3 feet (91cm) between plants. Keep well watered in periods of drought.

Pick leaves as you need them. In the proper conditions, the plant quickly regrows. 'Rubra', a handsome cultivar, has red stems and red-veined leaves.

Marionberry

Rubus occidentalis (Rosaceae)

Similar to loganberry, marionberry produces fruit for two months and is found predominantly in the Pacific Northwest. Allow 12 feet (3.7m) between these thorny plants. See Brambleberry (page 49) for cultivating tips.

Maypop

Passiflora incarnata (Passifloraceae)

Maypop is a perennial vine, root-hardy from Zones 5 to 10. Don't be mislead by the appearance of the plant; the stems die back to the ground each winter, but the roots are hardy, sending up new shoots in late spring. Maypop plants may need cross-pollination. Maypop bears white, pink, and purple flowers and yellow, egg-sized fruit. See Passionfruit (page 64) for cultivating tips.

MELON

Cucumis melo (Cucurbitaceae)

Melons are large fruits that are juicy summer treats. They grow on large vines in Zone 4 and warmer, needing 68 to 95 frost-free days to mature. For colder areas, try to plant only short-season cultivars.

All melons need full sun and good air circulation around the vines. They yield best when grown in well-drained soil amended with plenty of organic material, pH 6.0 to 7.0. Seed directly in the garden (or start indoors in cooler areas) in hills of three to four seeds, spaced 4 to 5 feet (1.2–1.5m) apart. Cultivate gently and shallowly until plant begins to vine. Feed weekly to keep vines strong and healthy. To minimize pests and diseases in the garden, avoiding planting where other melons, squash, gourds, or cucumbers have grown over the past three years. See also Apple Melon (page 46), Cantaloupe (page 51), Casaba Melon (page 51), Crenshaw Melon (page 52), Honeydew Melon (page 58), Muskmelon (below), and Watermelon (page 73).

Muscadine Grape

Vitis rotundifolia (Vitaceae)

Muscadine (or scuppernong) grapes are good for jam or jelly as well as eating out of hand. They have a unique musky flavor and grow in loose clusters. Tolerant of a lot of heat and humidity, they may need a pollinator, so carefully check the variety you choose. Perfect muscadine grapes, which do not require a pollinator: pink-blushed gold 'Carlos'; large bronze 'Fry'; black 'Hunt', suited for wine or grape juice; large black 'Jumbo'; disease-resistant 'Magoon'; and 'Scuppernong', the oldest grape cultivated in the United States, which is the premier muscadine to which all others are compared. See Grape (page 57) for cultivating tips.

Muskmelon

Cucumis melo, Reticulatus group (Cucurbitaceae)

Incorrectly called cantaloupe, muskmelon (also called Persian melon and nutmeg melon) is the melon we buy in the supermarket as the standard cantaloupe with ridged, netted rind and sweet orange flesh. 'Jenny Lind' is a favorite heirloom variety. See Melon (above) for cultivating tips.

PASSIONFRUIT

PASSIONFRUIT

Passiflora spp. (Passifloraceae)

Passionfruits are select members of the passionflower family that are grown for their edible fruits in addition to their striking flowers. With the exception of maypop, all are semitropical vines. The semitropical passionfruits bear fruit within one to two years after planting. Ripening from summer to late autumn, a mature plant can yield fifteen pounds (7kg) of fruit a year.

Passionfruit will thrive in most any garden soil in full sun when provided with good support—a strong trellis, fence, or a good-size shrub—for it to climb by its tendrils. Often suckers appear at the base of the mother plant; keep these pruned or the plant will quickly get out of hand. For the best quality and maximum fruit yield, hand-pollinate the flowers in late morning. Some varieties are self-pollinating. Be aware that other varieties, like 'Incense', are pollen-sterile and cannot be used as pollinators; enjoy these for the magnificent flowers.

The egg-shaped fruit are quite unusual. They separate easily from the vine, falling to the ground when ripe. Cut the top off the fruit and it appears to be filled with air and gloppy-looking seeds. The gelatinous material surrounding each seed is quite tasty, with a flavor reminiscent of fruit punch. See also Granadilla (page 56), Maypop (page 63), Purple Granadilla (page 67), and Yellow Granadilla (page 74).

Pea

Pisum sativum (Fabaceae)

Peas (also known as green peas, and garden peas, English peas, and shelling peas) are cool-weather, annual, vining vegetables. There is a wide range of varieties, from snow peas and sugar snaps, to traditional garden peas. Peas are fast-growing and -maturing, depending on the variety, in fifty-five to eighty days. Peas can grow from Zone 2 and warmer. They are attractive plants with blue-green, oval leaves 1 to 2 inches

PEA FLOWER

(2.5–5cm) long. They are true vines with tendrils that curl around objects to support themselves. Indeed, if you look at the plant from a different perspective than just an entity that produces podded legumes, you find that much of it is edible, with a distinctive pealike flavor. The young shoots, used in Asian cuisine, are delicious stir-fried or steamed. The tendrils themselves have been a little-known delicacy but are now gaining favor in nouvelle cuisine. They are excellent raw in salads or lightly cooked. The flowers are edible too. Remember, though, that picking the flowers will cut down on pea production. Sow a few more seeds to keep you in flowers, shoots, tendrils, and peas. Eat only true garden peas, *Pisum* species. Sweet peas, although they have attractive flowers, are poisonous.

Peas need full sun and sandy, well-drained soil with a pH between 6.0 and 7.0. Plant seeds directly in the garden as soon as the soil can be worked in the spring in cold areas (two to four weeks before the last frost date). In warm areas of the deep South and the West, plant peas in the fall or winter. For best results, soak the peas overnight in lukewarm water and roll them in a legume innoculant powder before planting. Space low-growing varieties of peas 1 to 2 inches (2.5–5cm) apart in rows 2 feet (61cm) apart, and tall varieties 3 feet (91.5cm) apart. A trellis or support must be at least as tall as the variety planted.

A daily harvest of peas will ensure an ongoing supply as the plant continues to flower. Shelling peas are best picked when the pods are plump and full. Snap peas should be picked when the pods are slightly rounded but still smooth. Snow peas are best picked while the pods are still completely flat, with only the suggestion of the peas inside. Eat, freeze, or can peas as soon as possible after picking, as the sugars quickly turn to starch. Peas that have gone past the picking stage should be allowed to dry; dried peas can be used like dried beans to flavor soups and stews.

Some of the best varieties include 'Burpeeana Early', 24 inches (61cm) tall; 'Maestro', 26 inches (66cm) tall, good fall crop; 'Wando', 30 inches (76cm) tall, heat-resistant; 'Daybreak', 20 inches (51cm) tall; 'Alaska', 3 to 4 feet (91.5cm to 1.2m) tall; 'Little Marvel', 15 inches (38cm) tall; 'Green Shaft', 30 inches (76cm) tall; 'Knight', 24 inches (61cm) tall; 'Puget', 32 inches (81.5cm) tall; 'Top Pod', 36 inches (91.5cm) tall; 'Leafless Pea Twiggy', 28 inches (71cm) tall (tendrils intertwine, eliminating need for trellising); 'Novella', 36 inches (91.5cm) tall (with numerous tendrils that intertwine with each other, this is a favorite of chefs who cook with tendrils); and 'Precovelle', French petit pois. See also Edible Podded Peas (page 54).

Pie Pumpkin

Cucurbita moschata (Cucurbitaceae)

Not surprisingly, these are the best pumpkins for pies. Choice cultivars include 'White Rind Sugar', solid flesh with white skin; 'Landreth Cheese', very dark orange, moist flesh; 'Baby Boo', 3-inch (7.5cm) ghost pumpkins with white skin; and 'Lumina', cream-colored skin, 10 pounds (4.5kg). See Pumpkin (below) for cultivating tips.

Pole Bean

Phaseolus vulgaris (Fabaceae)

A number of different types of string beans grow as long, vining plants requiring support. They are later to mature than bush string beans, but in generally continue to produce over a longer period of time. Some of the best choices include tender-crisp 'Blue Lake'; French pole filet bean 'Emerite'; the old favorite 'Kentucky Wonder', which is good fresh or dried and used as a shell bean; flat-podded Italian 'Romano', the exquisite shell bean 'Wren's Egg'; the unique curly podded 'Sultan's Emerald Crescent'; and the golden, twisted pods of 'Sultan's Golden Crescent'. See Bean (page 47) for cultivating tips.

Pumpkin

Cucurbita pepo var. *pepo* (Cucurbitaceae)

Pumpkins (also called jack-o'-lanterns and sugar pumpkins) are large, orange, furrowed fruits that grow on sprawling, prostrate, prickly stemmed vines with large, triangular, lobed leaves. They grow from Zone 4 and warmer. Pumpkins need 100 to 115 frost-free days to mature.

Pumpkins grow in full sun in most soil, as long as it is fertile with a pH between 6.0 and 7.0. Plant seeds outdoors, after all danger of frost has passed, in hills (two to three seeds per hill) spaced 4 to 5 feet (1.2–1.5m) apart. In cold areas, start the seeds indoors in peat pots two to three weeks before last frost date. Transplant into the garden after all danger of frost is past. Add some compost or organic matter to the hill to promote growth. Mulch well. Once the plant begins to leaf out, the large leaves will shade out most potential weeds. Pumpkin vines are vigorous, needing a lot of room to grow. If possible, plant in an area where they can sprawl without having to be concerned about their overrunning precious garden space.

Pick pumpkins when they have completely colored and the shell is hard. In most all cases, you can wait until a light frost has killed the vines before you pick the pumpkins. Store pumpkins in a cool, dry space. Pumpkins come in a range of sizes, adding to their versatility. 'Jack Be Little', a 3-inch (7.5cm) pumpkin, that can be trellised to grow vertically; 'Munchkin', 3-inch (7.5cm) pumpkins that can be grown on a trellis or up bean poles; 'Small Sugar', good for pies; 'Mini Jack', a small pumpkin with edible seeds; 'Autumn Gold Hybrid', 7- to 10-pound (3–4.5kg) pumpkins; 'Triple Treat', good for pies, seeds, and carving, 8 pounds (3.6kg); 'Jack-O'-Lantern', great carver; 'Ghost Rider', 20 pounds (9.1kg), cooking or carving; and 'Baby Bear', 4- to 6-inch (10–15cm) pumpkins good for pies. See also Giant Pumpkin (page 55), Japanese Pumpkin (page 60), and Pie Pumpkin (above).

'SCARLET RUNNER' BEAN

Purple Granadilla

Passiflora edulis (Passifloraceae)

Purple granadilla is a tropical vine that bears smallish white and purple flowers, which give rise to egg-sized, purple fruit. It is grown commercially in Australia. See Passionfruit (page 64) for cultivating tips.

Raspberry

Rubus spp. (Rosaceae)

There are two types of raspberries—black (*Rubus occidentalis*) and red (*R. ideaus*). Red raspberries are the hardiest of the brambleberries (some are hardy to Zone 3) and grow on upright canes or semitrailing vines. Black raspberries (hardy to Zone 5) grow in a similar fashion, but are more tender. Recommended varieties include midseason 'Citadel'; hardy 'Everbearing Fall Red'; delicious, everbearing 'Fall Gold'; burgundy-wine 'Killarney'; adaptable 'Latham'; and virus-free 'Taylor'. See Brambleberry (page 49) for cultivating tips.

Runner Bean

Phaseolus coccineus (Fabaceae)

Runner beans are perennial vines that are usually grown as annuals. The plants bear a resemblance to pole snap beans, but with darker green, denser leaves. The colorful flowers are edible, with a delicate beany flavor. If you are growing these plants for the flowers, the more you pick the more the plant will keep producing. However, beans will not form if the flowers are picked. Six to eight plants usually supply more than enough flowers for picking and allow for some to mature into beans. The young bean pods are dark green and straight. When cut cross-wise, they appear oval. For best eating, pick the pods when they are no more than 4 inches (10cm) long. As they grow bigger, they become stringy. As the pods age, the surface becomes striated. For

SQUASH BLOSSOM

dried beans, simply allow the pods to wither and then harvest the beans. All varieties are handsome ornamentals. Consider the red-orange-flowered 'Scarlet Runner'; white-flowered 'Dutch White'; the

showy coral and white flowers of the British heirloom 'Painted Lady'; and the smooth, stringless 'Red Knight'. See Bean (page 47) for more cultivating tips.

Serpent Gourd

Trichosanthes anguina (Cucurbitaceae)

A tall-growing annual vine, serpent gourd (also known as snake gourd and club gourd) bears white flowers followed by 1- to 5-foot (91.5cm–1.5m) long, slender, greenish-white fruit in varying shapes (cucumberlike, curved, club-shaped, or coiled). In India this gourd is used as a vegetable. Unlike other gourds, it does not dry well for ornamental purposes. See Gourd (page 55) for cultivating tips.

Spaghetti Squash

Cucurbita pepo (Cucurbitaceae)

Also called vegetable spaghetti, the ovoid winter-type spaghetti squash has light yellow skin and pale yellow flesh. Baked and scraped out, the flesh looks like yellow spaghetti. 'Vegetable Spaghetti' and 'Orangetti Hybrid' are good varieties. See Squash (below) for cultivating tips.

SQUASH

Cucurbita pepo (Cucurbitaceae)

Native Americans grew summer and winter squash long before the Spanish brought other varieties to North and South America. All squash are tender annuals. In general they are vining plants, and can grow to prodigious lengths, meandering through the garden. Varieties that produce smallish fruit can be trained on a trellis. Be sure that the squash, once formed, are supported from the sides and beneath. Old stockings make great support ties; the squash can cradle in the stretchy mesh.

In general, squash leaves are large and attractive. Grow the vines on a sunny hillside where they can run as much as they want, while providing needed erosion control and ground cover. Summer-type squash grow in Zones 3 and warmer, needing 42 to 65 frost-free days to reach maturity, while winter-type squash is better suited to Zones 4 and warmer, requiring 85 to 110 frost-free days; winter squash is also good for winter storage.

Squash grow best in full sun in rich, well-drained, humusy soil with pH 6.0 to 6.5. They need good air circulation to prevent disease. Summer squash grow so quickly that it is easiest to seed them directly into the garden once all danger of frost has passed. Squash that need a long growing season should be started indoors in the coldest areas. Black plastic mulch helps to warm the soil early in the season and keep out weeds, but do not use black plastic in warm climates. In warm areas, it pays to mulch, but choose an organic material such as grass clippings, hay, pine needles, or cocoa hulls. To meet squash's heavy nutrient needs, dig a hole about a foot deep and fill it with well-rotted manure or compost. Form a hill with the soil from the hole. Plant two or three seeds in the hole. Allow 4 feet (1.2m) between plants. Mulch with straw to hold in moisture and deter insects. Water well throughout the growing season. Side-dress several times with compost or well-rotted manure.

For best flavor, pick summer-type squash when it is small. Harvest often for continuous production. Cut the stem of the squash with a knife, being careful not to bruise the squash. Squash flowers are edible; they are delicious sautéed, stuffed and baked, or fried. Winter-type squash should be picked when the shell is tough enough that it does not dent when a fingernail is pushed against it. Harvest all winter-type squash as soon as the first light frost has killed the vines. Leave the squash on the ground to cure for ten to fourteen days, and cover at night with a blanket if frost threatens. To store, make a weak solution of bleach and water; wipe the squash with this to inhibit rot. Store in a cool, dry, well-ventilated space.

When buying seeds or plants, look for modern varieties that are labeled as disease-resistant. 'Gourmet Globe Hybrid' has attractive round, green-striped fruit with pale green flesh. In addition, some of the heirloom varieties, by virtue of the fact that they have been around for so long, perform

'GOURMET GLOBE HYBRID' SUMMER SQUASH

well, are disease-resistant, and more flavorful than the newer varieties. See also Buttercup Squash (page 50), Butternut Squash (page 50), Delicate Squash (page 54), Hubbard Squash (page 59), Kuta Hybrid Squash (page 61), Spaghetti Squash (page 68), Summer Squash (below), Sweet Dumpling Squash (page 70), Winter Squash (page 74), Yellow Squash (page 74), and Zucchini (page 74).

Summer Squash

Cucurbita pepo var. *melopepo* (Cucurbitaceae)

Also called patty pan squash, summer squash is noted for its flattish shape with scalloped edges. Select varieties include the following: 'Butter Scallop Hybrid', buttery yellow skin, creamy flesh; 'Sunburst Hybrid', bright yellow skin marked green at both ends; 'Peter Pan Hybrid', green fruit; and 'Wood's Earliest Prolific', strikingly white skin. See Squash (page 68) for cultivating tips.

Sunberry

Rubus hybrid (Rosaceae)

A very vigorous and spiny brambleberry, sunberry has dark red, loganberrylike fruit with great flavor. Allow 15 feet (4.6m) between plants. See Brambleberry (page 49) for cultivating tips.

Sweet Dumpling Squash

Cucurbita pepo (Cucurbitaceae)

Sweet dumpling squash has small, round, flattened fruit, pale and dark green striped skin, and light orange flesh. Unlike other winter-type squash, it needs no curing. The 'Sweet Mama Hybrid' (85 days) was an All-America Seeds winner. See Squash (page 68) for cultivating tips.

Sweet Potato

Ipomoea batatas (Convolvulaceae)

Sweet potatoes are frost-tender, warm-weather, perennial, running plants grown for their sweet, orange-fleshed, tuberous roots. They grow in Zones 5 and warmer, requiring 90 to 120 frost-free days to produce good tubers.

Sweet potatoes need full sun and deeply cultivated, loose, well-drained soil with pH 5.5 to 6.5. After all danger of frost has passed and the soil has warmed, plant the "slips" (growing shoots available by mail-order, and at nurseries and garden centers). Form a ridge of soil about 8 to 10 inches (20.5–25.5cm) high and 8 inches (20.5cm) wide. Plant the slips in the ridge, spaced 12 inches (30.5cm) apart. After several weeks, mound soil onto the ridge; if possible, repeat again. Keep evenly moist until the slips begin to grow, then water only during drought.

Gently dig the sweet potatoes before hard frost or after the vines have died back. Handle with care, as they bruise easily. Cure for about two weeks in a warm, humid location, then store above 55 degrees F (12.8°C). Once cooked, they freeze well.

'VARDAMAN' SWEET POTATO

TAYBERRY

Dry-flesh varieties are usually called sweet potatoes, including 'Orlis' and 'Yellow Jersey'. Moist-flesh varieties are incorrectly referred to as yams, including 'Georgia Jet', 'Vardaman', and 'Centennial'.

Tayberry

Rubus hybrid (Rosaceae)

Hybrids of red raspberries and blackberries and larger than loganberries, deep purple tayberries have a sweet, firm, juicy fruit. Allow 8 feet (2.4m) between plants. See Brambleberry (page 49) for cultivating tips.

Tomato

Lycopersicon esculentum (Solanaceae)

Tomatoes (also known as love apples, golden apples, and pomos d'oro) are vining plants that are grown for their fruit, which range far beyond the standard tennis ball–sized round red fruit. They come in many colors and range from grape-size to grapefruit-size. Nothing can match the flavor of a home-grown tomato, whatever the variety. Tomatoes are either determinate or indeterminate. Determinate vines grow only to a certain length, and the main stem develops a flower bud at the top of its growth. Determinate tomatoes include the so-called bush tomatoes and many of the early season varieties. All of the tomatoes tend to ripen at once. Determinate tomatoes are an excellent choice when space is at a premium and when you are trying to grow the plants in a cold climate with a short growing season. The main stem or terminal leader of indeterminate tomatoes does not develop a flower bud. Flower and fruit production continues as long as the growing conditions permit. The obvious advantage is that indeterminate tomatoes will keep on producing until the weather gets too cold. The disadvantage is that the plant can get very tall and rangy, needing caging or staking. Tomatoes grow in Zone 3 and warmer, requiring 52 to 90 frost-free days (from time of transplanting) to mature.

'GARDENER'S DELIGHT' TOMATO

Tomatoes need full sun and deeply cultivated, well-drained soil that has been amended with organic matter. Start tomato seeds indoors six to ten weeks before the last spring frost date. Start the seeds in 3-inch (7.5cm) peat pots. Fill the pots one-third full with sterile seed-starting mix. Place several seeds in the pot and cover with ½ inch (1.2cm) of mix. Cover pots with clear plastic and keep warm until seeds germinate, then place in full sun. As seedlings grow, gradually pinch off lower leaves and bury the stem by adding more soil. Roots form along the buried stem, making a stronger plant. After all danger of frost has passed and the ground has warmed, transplant tomatoes outdoors, allowing 24 inches (61cm) between plants. Again, remove all but the top four or five leaves and bury the stem. Place a stake or cage at the same time as planting so as not to disrupt the root system. Keep plants well watered. Fertilize with manure tea or fish emulsion when plants begin to flower. Mulch once soil is warm.

Pick tomatoes as they ripen. Eat them right off the vine or use raw in salads and sandwiches, or cook them, depending on the variety. With a food dehydrator (or an oven set at a very low temperature) you can make "sun-dried tomatoes" to enjoy through the winter. Pick all tomatoes before the first hard frost. Brought inside and wrapped in newspaper, some will ripen (others will rot), but they do not keep for long.

Beefsteak tomatoes are indeterminate, with large fruit up to 2 pounds (0.9kg) 'Beefmaster', 'Burpee's Supersteak Hybrid', 'Pink Ponderosa', 'Giant Belgium', 'Delicious', 'Super Beefsteak VFN', 'Bragger', 'Old Flame' (formerly 'Olympic Flame').

Cherry tomatoes have numerous 1-inch (1.2cm) fruits, usually in grape-like clusters. Select varieties include 'Sweet 100', indeterminate, red; 'Gold Nugget', determinate, yellow-orange; 'Green Grape', determinate, green-yellow; and 'Gardener's Delight', indeterminate, red.

Currant tomatoes are species tomatoes native to Central America, with tiny, currant-size fruit. 'Red' and 'Yellow' varieties are indeterminant and can run rampant. Children love them.

Low-acid tomatoes, which feature mild flavor and reduced acidity, are often yellow-skinned. Choice varieties include 'Pink Girl', indeterminate,

Standard tomatoes include all the other tomatoes that are grown to use fresh. There is an enormous choice of size, color, disease resistance, and type of vine. Noteworthy examples of the standard tomato include 'Early Girl', early, small, red; 'Big Boy Hybrid', large, red; 'Celebrity', disease-resistant, large, red; 'Jubilee', large, yellow-orange; 'Burpee's VF Hybrid', disease-resistant, red; 'Lady Luck Hybrid', disease-resistant, large, red; 'Heinz 1350', good for canning, red; 'Rutgers', an old standard; 'Dona', disease-resistant, red; 'Golden Mandarin Cross', deep, golden orange; 'Pink Odoriko', Japanese, deep rose-red; 'White Beauty', pale colored; 'Evergreen', green when ripe; and 'Striped Cavern', bicolor hollow tomato ideal for stuffing.

Tummelberry

Rubus hybrid (Rosaceae)

Tummelberry is a hybrid of tayberry, and a hardier plant. It has a sharp-flavored fruit. Allow eight feet (2.4m) between plants. See Brambleberry (page 49) for cultivating tips.

Vegetable Marrow Squash

Cucurbita pepo var. *pepo* (Cucurbitaceae)

Also called Lebanese zucchini, vegetable marrow squash is a dense 8- to 12-inch (20.5–30.5cm) fruit that is used like summer squash. 'Vegetable Marrow Bush' and 'Cousa' are two commonly grown varieties. See Squash (page 68) for cultivating tips.

Watermelon

Citrullus lanatus (Cucurbitaceae)

Watermelon is the classic sweet, juicy, pink-to-red (now yellow, too) fleshed melon of summer, with dark to light green rind that may be striped, mottled, or solid in color. Choice varieties include heirloom 'Moon

'SWEET FAVORITE' WATERMELON

pink; 'Lemon Boy', indterminate, yellow; 'Jetstar', determinate, red; 'Orange Boy', indeterminate, orange; and 'Mr. Stripey', yellow with pink stripes.

Traditionally used for sauce, paste tomatoes, with drier pulp and fewer seeds, are often plum-shaped and determinate. Examples include 'Roma', small; 'Milano', early; 'Royal Chico', large; and 'San Marzano', large and meaty.

Patio tomatoes are determinate varieties bred to be grown in containers. They are a boon to small gardens too. Recommended are 'Patio'; 'Better Bush'; 'Pixie Hybrid II', 'Orange Pixie Hybrid VFT', disease-resistant, orange; 'Basket King Hybrid', good for hanging baskets; and 'Micro-Tom', a miniature vine.

Pear tomatoes are small tomatoes with a pear shape. The plants are red- and yellow-fruited indeterminate vines.

'CREAM OF THE CROP HYBRID' WINTER SQUASH

and Stars', 'Sugar Baby', Charleston Gray', 'Yellow Baby', and 'Black Diamond'. See Melon (page 63) for cultivating tips.

Winter Squash

Cucurbita pepo var. *pepo* (Cucurbitaceae)

Also known as acorn or pepper squash, winter squash is an acorn-shaped squash with dark green skin and moist, sweet orange flesh. The best varieties are 'Cream of the Crop Hybrid', with creamy white skin, and 'Early Acorn Hybrid'. See Squash (page 68) for cultivating tips.

Yellow Granadilla

Passiflora laurifolia (Passifloraceae)

Native to South America, yellow granadilla (also known as water-lemon and Jamaican honeysuckle) bears white flowers with red and purple spots and yellow fruit. See Passionfruit (page 64) for cultivating tips.

Yellow Squash

Cucurbita pepo var. *melopepo* (Cucurbitaceae)

This summer type is a long, yellow-skinned squash with off-white flesh. Recommended varieties include 'Seneca Butterbar Hybrid'; 'Dixie Hybrid', small yellow crookneck; and 'Golden Early Summer Crookneck', yellow crookneck. See Squash (page 68) for cultivating tips.

Zucchini

Cucurbita pepo var. *melopepo* (Cucurbitaceae)

A summer standard, zucchini has long, green fruit with creamy-white flesh. The best varieties include 'Seneca Milano'; 'Gold Rush', yellow skin; and Park's 'Green Whopper'. See Squash (page 68) for cultivating tips.

ORNAMENTALS: ANNUAL AND TENDER PERENNIAL VINES

Black-Eyed Susan Vine

Thunbergia alata (Acanthaceae)

Native to tropical Africa, the blue trumpet vine tender perennial (most commonly grown as an annual) is a twining vine growing to 8 feet (2.4m). It can be grown as a perennial in Zones 9 and 10, but any frost will kill the plant completely. The coarsely toothed, triangular, medium-green leaves are a good backdrop for the vivid blooms. From a distance, the flowers look like little daisies. Up close, each bright orange flower is a narrow trumpet that flares broadly. Viewed straight on, the flower looks flat; the center of the trumpet is black, creating this optical illusion.

After all danger of frost has passed, plant outdoors in full sun in well-drained, moist soil amended with plenty of organic matter. You can find small plants at nurseries and garden centers, or start the vine from seed. Eight weeks before the last frost date, sow seeds indoors in individual peat pots about ¼ inch (6mm) deep. Keep in partial shade until the seeds germinate, then move into full sun. In warm climates, sow the seeds directly in the garden about the time of the last frost. Train the vines to climb wires, strings, or a trellis. In a pot, black-eyed Susan vine makes an impressive hanging basket. Use the vine to hide an eyesore—place a planted container on top of an old tree stump and let the leaves and the flowers cascade down. Several varieties are available, with all-yellow blooms and white flowers with black throats.

Blue Moonflower

Ipomoea indica (Convolvulaceae)

This vine (also called dawnflower) grows to 35 feet (10.5m) tall, with 4-inch (10cm), deep violet flowers with bands of lighter blue and a white throat. See Morning Glory (page 80) for cultivating tips.

BLACK-EYED SUSAN VINE

Blue Trumpet Vine

Thunbergia grandiflora (Acanthaceae)

The botanical name says it all: the blue trumpet vine is a large-flowered thunbergia. Its 3-inch (7.5cm), sky-blue flowers have given rise to many common names: clock vine, blue clock vine, Bengal clock vine, sky vine, skyflower, and blue skyflower. It is a woody twining vine, with large, 8-inch (20.5cm) leaves. The flowers are borne in large drooping racemes, usually opening one or two at a time from the top down. Hardy in Zones 8 to 10, it makes a spectacular container plant in cooler areas. Place the pot next to a small trellis, or allow the vine to climb a drain pipe. 'Alba' has white flowers. See Black-Eyed Susan Vine (page 75) for cultivating tips.

Brazilian Morning Glory

Ipomoea setosa (Convolvulaceae)

Ten-inch (25cm), grapelike leaves with three lobes distinguish this morning glory. Rosy purple flowers open from mid- to late August and continue until frost on this 30-foot (9m) vine. See Morning Glory (page 80) for cultivating tips.

Canary-Bird Flower

Tropaeolum peregrinum (Tropaeolaceae)

Also known as canary creeper, this annual vine grows to 10 feet (3m). The pale green leaves are reminiscent of nasturtium (to which this plant is related) but with five deeply cut lobes. Throughout the summer, the vine produces uniquely fringed yellow flowers that, from a distance, resemble small canaries. Unlike nasturtiums, canary-bird flower thrives in partial shade in rich soil. Keep the vine well watered throughout the growing season. See Nasturtium (page 81) for cultivating tips.

Chickabiddy

Asarina antirrhinifolia (Scrophulariaceae)

A southwestern American native that grows wild from Texas to California and Mexico, the twining climber known as chickabiddy (or climbing snapdragon) is a tender perennial that will grow to 10 feet (3m). It is related to snapdragons. A genteel vine in contrast to the many rampant vines, chickabidy makes a perfect accent plant, trellised in a container (even trained to climb up string) or on a porch railing. The foliage resembles English ivy, with 1- to 2-inch (2.5–5cm), heart-shaped leaves. The flowers are the main attraction. Funnel-shaped and 2 inches (5cm) long, they range in hue from rosy pink to reddish purple. Chickabiddy can bloom from June through the summer, continuing until a killing frost.

Plant in full sun to light shade. Chickabiddy grows best in rich, moist, well-drained soil, but will tolerate less optimum soil. Start seeds indoors in late winter or early spring for summer bloom.

Chilean Glory Flower

Eccremocarpus scaber (Bignoniaceae)

Native to Chile, Chilean glory flower (also known as Chilean glory vine or glory flower), a hardy perennial vine, is an annual in areas where winter temperatures drop below 32 degrees F (0°C) for any length of time. Climbing by tendrils, it grows to 12 feet (3.7m). Satiny, bright green, compound leaves are made up of ½- to 1-inch (1.2–2.5cm) leaflets. The 1-inch (2.5cm), trumpet-shaped flowers in hues of yellow, orange, and red are borne in clusters that bloom from late spring into fall. This is one of the fastest-growing vines from seed to flower. Chilean glory flower is exquisite trained up an arbor, pergola, trellis, or even on a simple wire or string grid as a seasonal screen.

Choose a sunny warm spot with fertile, well-drained soil for the best flowering; however, it is tolerant of less favorable conditions. For gardeners who are hesitant to grow plants from seed, this is the one to grow. In the coldest areas, start the seeds indoors in peat pots two months before the last frost date. The seedlings do not transplant well, so the peat pots can go directly into the ground without disturbing the seedlings or their roots at all. In warmer climates, sow directly in the garden when all danger of frost has passed and the soil has warmed. In the mildest areas, where it is grown as a perennial, cut the plant back to several inches in late fall or early spring. This hard pruning will rejuvenate the vine.

Creeping Gloxinia

Asarina erubescens (Scrophulariaceae)

Native to Mexico, creeping gloxinia is a twining climber that grows only about 6 feet (1.8m) tall. Leaves are 1½ to 3 inches (4–7.5cm) long and shiny. The rosy pink flowers are 2 to 3 inches (5–7.5cm) long with notched lobes. See Chickabiddy (page 76) for cultivating tips.

Cup-and-Saucer Vine

Cobaea scandens (Polemoniaceae)

Native to Mexico, the cup-and-saucer vine, a tender perennial, has several common names that reflect its heritage and appearance, among them Mexican ivy and monastery-bells. Its botanical name calls to mind the seventeenth-century Spanish naturalist and Jesuit missionary, Father Cobo. Whatever you want to call it, cup-and-saucer vine is a lovely plant whose tendrils can curl around an arbor or pergola, creating welcome shade. Fast growing, it can easily reach 25 feet (7.5m). The compound leaves are made up of four to six oval, dull green, 4-inch (10cm) leaflets. From midsummer to killing frost, the vine blooms with flowers that are greenish-white in bud, turning violet to deep purple as they open. The 2-inch (5cm), bell-shaped corolla is set on a saucerlike calyx, giving rise to the plant's most common name. Plumlike, insignificant fruits follow the flowers. 'Alba' has white flowers.

Plant in full sun, except in the warmest climates, where it needs protection from midday scalding. In warm areas, plant it against an east- or south-facing wall. It prefers rich, well-drained, moist soil amended with plenty of organic

CUP-AND-SAUCER VINE

matter. In areas with mild winters, grow the vine as a perennial; hard frost kills the roots, so it must be grown as an annual elsewhere. Start the seeds indoors two months before the last frost. Mix light potting soil with vermiculite and fill small pots with the mixture. Place the seed on its edge and gently push it into the soil mix so only the top of the seed is exposed. Once the seedlings have developed at least two true leaves, and all danger of frost has passed, plant out into the garden. Keep the plants evenly moist. When grown as a perennial, cup-and-saucer vine may require pruning to keep it in control and well trained. Otherwise, pinch the growing tips of the vine to create a bushy effect.

Cypress Vine

Ipomoea quamoclit (Convolvulaceae)

Lovely, delicate fernlike foliage and small (1½ inches [4cm]), brilliant scarlet flowers distinguish the lovely cypress vine. The vine grows to 20 feet (6m). Flowers close when direct sun is on them; they open widely at sundown and in the early morning. Grow it where you can appreciate the fine form of the leaves. See Morning Glory (page 80) for cultivating tips.

Horsfall Morning Glory

Ipomoea horsfalliae briggsii (Convolvulaceae)

In Zone 10, grow this magnificent vine outdoors; it will bloom twice, in early winter and again in early summer, bearing 2½-inch (6.5cm), crimson-magenta blooms. Deeply cut, glossy dark green foliage covers this 40-foot (12.2m) vine. See Morning Glory (page 80) for cultivating tips.

Japanese Morning Glory

Ipomoea nil (Convolvulaceae)

Japanese morning glories are the largest-flowered of the many species of morning glory. Deeply cut leaves cover the 20-foot (6m) vine. See Morning Glory (page 80) for cultivating tips.

CYPRESS VINE

Moonflower

Ipomoea alba (Convolvulaceae)

Native to tropical America, the vigorous moonflower vine is technically a tender perennial, but it is commonly grown as an annual. A night-blooming cousin of morning glory, this twining vine with wiry stems can grow to 40 feet (12m), given the proper conditions. It thrives in hot weather, and is slow to get going if the temperature is below 70 degrees F (21.1°C). Soft green, heart-shaped leaves make this an attractive vine even before it starts to flower. In midsummer (sometimes later, depending on the weather), the vine begins to bloom. At first only one, and then several, flowers open each night. Within a couple of weeks, the vine is covered with broadly opened, almost iridescent, satiny white blooms 5 to 6 inches (12.5–15cm) across. The vine continues to produce flowers until the first frost, when it dies to

MOONFLOWER

the ground. The flower's fragrance is alluring, both to humans and to the plant's night pollinators. With luck, you may see a luna moth or other magnificent creature of the night at work. Each flower stays open for a single night, lasting through the night and closing when sunlight shines directly on it. On cloudy days the flowers may stay open. Each night there are new flowers to replace the ones that bloomed the previous night.

Although they are tender perennials, moonflowers are usually grown as annuals from seed. Some nurseries have seedlings available in early summer, but it is easier and more economical to start the seed yourself. Plant the seeds indoors in peat pots, or seed directly in the garden once the soil temperature is above 70 degrees F (21.1°C). First, soak the seeds overnight in tepid water. With a knife, score or nick the seed coat. Plant the seeds ½ inch (1.2cm) deep in rich, well-drained, moist soil in full sun. The seeds can be slow to germinate. Provide strong support in the form of a trellis, fence, post, or arbor. The vines make a beautiful screen to shade a sunny room in summer. Grow moonflowers where you can appreciate the magnificent blooms.

Morning Glory

Ipomoea purpurea (Convolvulaceae)

This large genus includes more than five hundred species and related plants. All the morning glories included here are twining, tender (frost-sensitive) annuals. Morning glories are the most popular annual vines grown in America because of their beauty, ease of growing, and reliability. Typically, morning glories have large, heart-shaped, medium green leaves and funnel-shaped flowers. The flowers, which may be up to 5 inches (12.5cm) across, open the first thing in the morning and close by midday. Each flower lasts only a single day, and there are always buds developing, waiting to be the next morning's glory. Flowers range from solid hues of pink, white, crimson, purple, and blue to bicolors and double-flowering varieties. Morning glory vines grow to 10 feet (3m) or more. They are easily supported by strings attached to the eaves, on trellises, around a gazebo, on

MORNING GLORY

a chain-link fence, or almost anywhere they can twine. Plant them around the base of your compost bin for a beautiful, flowering screen.

Morning glories grow best in full sun in rich, well-drained soil. They are drought-tolerant and will grow in almost any soil. They put out a great deal of energy in flowering every day, and appreciate a feeding with fish emulsion every two weeks. Morning glories are readily grown from seed; few are available as transplants in nurseries or garden centers. Before planting, soak the seeds overnight in tepid water. Sow the seeds ½ inch (1.2cm) deep outdoors after all danger of frost has passed, or indoors a month earlier in individual peat pots. Space plants about 12 inches (30.5cm) apart.

Some of the named varieties include 'Giant Cornell', carnelian with white edge; large white 'Pearly Gates'; rosy red 'Scarlett O'Hara'; and 'Darling', a wine-red with a white throat.

Ipomoea tricolor includes some of the favorite morning glory hybrids: the classic 'Heavenly Blue', with sky-blue flowers and white throats; light sky-blue 'Summer Skies'; rosy lavender 'Wedding Bells'; and striped sky-blue-and-white 'Flying Saucers'. See also Blue Moonflower (page 75), Brazilian Morning Glory (page 76), Cypress Vine (page 78), Horsfall Morning Glory (page 78), and Japanese Morning Glory (page 78).

Nasturtium

Tropaeolum majus (Tropaeolaceae)

Nasturtium (also called garden or climbing nasturtium) is a member of a large genus that includes about fifty species of annuals and perennials, most of which are climbers native to South America. The garden nasturtium is the most commonly grown, prized for its brightly colored red, orange, or yellow flowers and rounded green leaves. New introductions have flowers of mahogany, cream, pink, and even speckled flowers. The peppery flavor of the leaves and flowers is a great addition to salads and sandwiches. Use flowers from several different varieties tossed with a mix of lettuces for an elegant, tasty salad.

A tender annual, nasturtium grows best in full sun in ordinary garden soil. In warmer areas, they prefer light shade. Soil that is too rich will result in lots of leaves and few, if any, flowers. Nasturtium thrives in relatively cool weather, and cannot tolerate the heat of the South in summer, yet they are drought-tolerant. Even in the Northeast, they fade in July and August, only to revive as the days cool in September. In California, if the winter is mild enough, the plants can survive if there is no killing frost. Nasturtium is easy to grow from seed, needing cool soil to germinate. Sow the seeds directly in the garden two weeks before the last frost date in spring. Space plants at least a foot (30.5cm) apart. Cover with ½ inch (1.2cm) of soil and water well. Seeds can also be sown indoors in individual peat pots.

NASTURTIUM

SWEET PEA

True climbing varieties can reach 6 to 10 feet (1.8–3m), happily trailing along the ground or climbing up a trellis. Newer hybrids are more compact, spreading 12 to 18 inches (30.5–46cm).

'Empress of India' has brilliant vermilion-red flowers that contrast with its deep blue-green foliage; 'Whirlybird' has dark green foliage, upward-facing, spurless, semidouble flowers of tangerine, salmon, bright gold, deep mahogany, bright scarlet, and cherry rose; 'Peach Melba' flower petals are the color of a sliced white peach with raspberry markings at the throat; 'Semi-Tall Double Gleam' is a trailing variety that spreads to 3 feet (91.5cm) with large, fragrant double and semidouble flowers; 'Fordhook Favorites Mixed' is a vigorous climber that reaches 6 feet (1.8m) in length, with single flowers in a good range of colors.

Orange Clockvine

Thunbergia gregorii (Acanthaceae)

A South African native, orange clockvine is a tender perennial related to the black-eyed Susan vine; it is grown as an annual in all but Zones 9 and 10. A twining climber, it can reach to 20 feet (6m), but is more restrained as a ground cover, growing to 5 feet (1.5m). The stems are hairy, as are the 3-inch (7.5cm), heart-shaped leaves. The intensely colored, pure orange flowers are produced in abundance from early spring to fall (throughout the summer in cooler climates). Give this vine a special place of its own; the flower color can be hard to blend with other plants. Train it up a fence or trellis, use as ground cover on a slope or rocky bank, or grow in a hanging basket. See Black-Eyed Susan Vine (page 75) for cultivating tips.

Sweet Pea

Lathyrus odoratus (Fabaceae)

Sweet peas, native to Italy, have been cultivated almost as long as roses—for thousands of years. This vining annual climbs by tendrils to a height of 7 feet (2m), with cultivated varieties that range from 2 to 6 feet (61cm–1.8m). The grayish-green, compound leaves are oval, making a handsome backdrop for the colorful blooms. The flowers look like garden pea flowers (they are members of the same family), but this plant is poisonous. The 2-inch (5cm) flowers are usually borne in clusters of three to five. Colors range through tones of scarlet, crimson, rose, salmon, medium blue, light blue, lavender, and white. The purple flowers of the old-fashioned cultivars are most fragrant. The unique scent of sweet pea, honey-like with a citrus overtone, is a delightful addition to any spring garden.

Like peas, the sweet pea is a cool-season plant that thrives in spring, but begins to fade as the mercury climbs. Sow seeds outdoors as soon as the soil can be worked in spring. To lengthen the season, apply a mulch of clear plastic over previously prepared soil in late winter. Plant the seeds through slits in the plastic. Allow four to six seeds per foot (30.5cm). When plants are about 2 inches (5cm) high, cover the plastic with grass clippings. In mild areas plant the seeds in late fall for spring bloom. Provide support for most varieties. Sweet peas are lovely climbing up any kind of trellis, formal or informal. The flowers are excellent cut flowers, long-lasting and fragrant. Choose from among the numerous cultivated varieties that include dwarf, heat-resistant, nonclimbing, and early-flowering types.

ORNAMENTALS: HARDY PERENNIAL AND WOODY VINES

Algerian Ivy

Hedera canariensis (Araliaceae)

Algerian ivy is hardy in Zones 8 to 10, and is used mostly as a ground cover. It is a handsome vine with large, 5- to 7-inch (12.7–17.8cm) leaves with distinctive red stems. 'Variegata' is a beautiful variegated form. See English Ivy (page 96) for cultivation tips.

American Bittersweet

Celastrus scandens (Celastraceae)

American bittersweet, a native of eastern North America, is distinguished by its oval, light green, 4-inch (10.2cm) leaves. The fruit is held in terminal clusters above the leaves. Hardier than Oriental bittersweet, it grows in Zones 3 to 9. It is a bit less aggressive than its cousin, growing only 10 to 20 feet (3–6.1m). See Bittersweet (page 84) for cultivation tips.

Angel Wing Jasmine

Jasminum nitidum (Oleaceae)

Hardy only in Zone 10, angel wing jasmine blooms in late spring and summer, perfuming California and southern gardens. It is an ideal plant for desert conditions, blooming profusely when the temperatures stay warm during its long growing season. When temperatures drop below 32 degrees F (0°C), it loses its leaves, but the roots will survive temperatures to 25 degrees F (-3.9°C). Angel wing jasmine grows moderately to a height of 10 to 20 feet (3–6.1m). The stems weakly twine and need support to grow vertically. The fragrant, 1- to 1½-inch (2.5 to 3.8cm), pinwheel-like flowers are borne in clusters of three on slender stalks. The flowers are white above, with purplish undersides. Leaves are glossy, 3-inch (7.6cm) ovals that are a lovely backdrop

AMERICAN BITTERSWEET

for the flowers. This jasmine makes a spectacular specimen plant. Tie it to an arbor or trellis, or use it against a fence. See Jasmine (page 102) for cultivation tips.

Arabian Jasmine

Jasminum sambac (Oleaceae)

Arabian jasmine probably originated in tropical Asia, but it has been cultivated for thousands of years, and its history has been forgotten. It is one of the oldest jasmine species in cultivation. Arabian jasmine is evergreen with slightly downy stems. The deep green leaves are opposite, sometimes in leaflets of three. The tubular, white flowers, borne in clusters in the winter, are intensely fragrant. The sweet-flavored flowers are traditionally used for scenting tea. 'Maid of Orleans' is an excellent new cultivar. See Jasmine (page 102) for cultivation tips.

Aralia Ivy

× *Fatshedera lizei* (*Fatsia japonica* × *Hedera helix*) (Araliaceae)

Aralia ivy, or fatshedera, is a genus that was created in 1911 when Lize Freres crossed plants of two different genera: Japanese aralia (*Fatsia japonica*) and English ivy (*Hedera helix*). The resulting plant is a genetic combination of the two parents, and its name combines both too. Aralia ivy has a number of common names, all of which make reference to its beginnings: botanical wonder, tree ivy, and ivy tree. Fatshedera is a semi-erect shrub with long, ropelike branches that need support to remain upright. If the tips of the branches are pinched back, the plant takes on a shrubby look like its aralia parent. Hardy in Zones 9 and 10, it is grown for its luxuriant evergreen foliage, rather than the greenish-white flowers that bloom in autumn. The large, glossy, dark green, deeply lobed, pointed leaves reach 5 to 9 inches (12.7– 22.9cm) in length and width.

Plant fatshedera in full sun to deep shade in coastal areas; in dry, hot areas it requires some shading and protection from the wind. Grow it in well-drained, moist soil. Feed in spring and summer to promote luxuriant growth. Pinching the growing tips encourages branching at the base. To use fatshedera as a ground cover, prune the laterals throughout the growing season and secure long branches to the ground. It is excellent trained against a fence, giving a rich, tropical feel to an area while providing a lush, green background for other flowering plants.

BITTERSWEET

Celastrus spp. (Celastraceae)

Bittersweets are hardy, vigorous, twining, deciduous, woody vines that can easily run rampant. They are grown for the attractive fruit that abound in autumn, persisting even after the leaves have fallen. Their long-lasting quality make the fruiting branches a favorite of flower arrangers. Bittersweets are dioecious, needing both male and female vines in close proximity for good fruit set. Inconspicuous white flowers appear in spring, followed by green fruit in summer on female plants. The small green fruit mature to yellow-orange, and burst open to reveal scarlet berries. Roundish, light green leaves turn bright yellow before falling in autumn.

Bittersweets are nothing if not adaptable, growing in full sun to partial shade, and tolerant of cold winters, high winds, drought, and most soil types (they thrive in poor, sandy soil, but languish in boggy, wet soil). They will grow in warmer climates, but require winter chill for a good fruit set.

In spring, before the leaves appear, give bittersweets a severe pruning. This will not only help keep the plants in control, preventing tangling, but encourage fruiting as flowering occurs on new wood. With judicious pruning, bittersweets are lovely covering an arbor, fence, or sturdy trellis. They make an effective ground cover in open spaces, as the branches circle around themselves, forming a dense, mounded mat. Keep bittersweets away from trees and shrubs, which they readily climb; their strong, twining habit eventually strangles the support plant. See also American Bittersweet (page 83) and Oriental Bittersweet (page 105).

BOUGAINVILLEA

Blood-Red Trumpet Vine

Distictis buccinatoria (Bignoniaceae)

Blood-red trumpet vine deserves a special place in the garden to show it off properly. The 4-inch (10.2cm) long, yellow-throated, scarlet flowers are held out from the foliage. As the flowers mature, they fade to rose red and then drop off the vine. In the warmest areas they can bloom almost non-stop. Two-inch (5.1cm) oval leaves are handsome on the twining branches. See Trumpet Vine (page 111) for cultivation tips.

Boston Ivy

Parthenocissus tricuspidata (Vitaceae)

A woodbine, Boston ivy is sometimes confused with English ivy, but in autumn it is obvious to anyone which is which. Boston ivy turns brilliant scarlet and yellow before the leaves drop off. The mesh of branches and the persistent blue berries give the vine winter interest. In spring the new leaves are purplish, maturing to large, tri-lobed leaves that can be 8 inches (20.3cm) wide. The leaves, borne on long stems, stand out from the branches, gracefully fluttering in the breeze.

Boston ivy is more tenacious and has a more branching habit than Virginia creeper, allowing it to cover large walls easily. It is a tough vine, thriving in cities, climbing up apartment house walls, unmindful of pollution. It softens the look of whatever it covers, even ugly tenements; think what it can do for a nice house or fence. 'Lowii', Low's creeper, has small leaves on short stalks, with restrained growth. 'Veitchii', Veitch's creeper, has very dainty leaves. See Woodbine (page 115) for cultivation tips.

Bougainvillea

Bougainvillea spp. (Nyctaginaceae)

Bougainvillea (or paper flower) is one of the showiest of the flowering vines. Semi-evergreen, the two species that are generally cultivated are

Bougainvillea glabra, with long-lasting flowers and a less vigorous habit, and *B. spectabilis*, showier and more tolerant of cool temperatures. Both are native to Brazil and are tender, growing best in Zones 9 and 10. The brightly colored parts of the plant are not flowers, but are made up of three showy bracts (specialized leaves, such as the colored portions of poinsettias and dogwoods, that are often mistaken for flowers) that surround very small, white flowers. The bract colors are vivid: hot pink, magenta, crimson, bronze, yellow, orange, and white of varying hues. The vines often bloom almost year-round, especially in the warmest regions. The heart-shaped leaves add interest when the bracts fade.

Bougainvillea thrives in full sun in well-drained garden soil. Soil that is too rich promotes luxuriant foliage at the expense of flower and bract formation. Plant bougainvillea in the spring, so that the plant is well established before cool weather sets in. Choose a location where the roots can spread out, and where they can be warmed by the heat of the sun or radiant heat from a wall, building, or patio. Bougainvillea is fussy about having its roots disturbed, so be very gentle when planting. Instead of tamping the plant out of its pot (as you would any other plant), carefully cut the bottom of the container away and set the plant in the hole. Then cut the container vertically in three or more places, peeling away the sides, and fill the hole with soil. Water it deeply until it gets established and sets out new growth. To encourage flowering, cut back to minimal watering. An evenly balanced organic fertilizer is optional in the spring.

A healthy bougainvillea is a large, heavy, twining vine with robust, thorned stems that require sturdy support. For that reason, you often see bougainvillea trained to grow up one side of a wall and cascade over the top, or up and over a pergola. Fasten the vine well to the support. Individual branches may also need tying to keep them from whipping in the wind and shredding their leaves. Heavy pruning will keep a bougainvillea within bounds. It can be cut back completely in spring and autumn, and will grow back and bloom the following season. Keep suckers pruned back and long branches removed to maintain shape while keeping overall plant volume and weight down.

CAPE HONEYSUCKLE

Cape Grape

Rhoicissus capensis (Vitaceae)

A tendril climber native to South Africa, the evergreen cape grape (also called evergreen grape or African grape) is hardy only in Zone 10. It is a handsome plant that resembles a grapevine. A moderate- to slow-growing vine, it can grow to 50 feet (15.2m), but 30 feet (9m) is more common. The long, branched tendrils form a green blanket when trained on a fence or lattice. Insignificant flowers bloom in spring, followed by shiny, reddish-black fruit that can be cooked or made into preserves. Despite the edibility of the fruit, this vine is grown mainly as an ornamental. The large, round to kidney-shaped leaves are bronzy in spring, maturing to a bright, shiny green. Leaves can grow 4 to 8 inches (10.2–20.3cm) long, with rusty hairs on the undersides, adding dimensional interest to the vine.

Cape grape is somewhat fussy; like clematis, it prefers its roots shaded, and its foliage in light. Plant the large, 6- to 8-inch (15.2–20.3cm) tubers in rich, well-drained loam. To keep the soil evenly moist, mulch with 2 to 3 inches (5.1–7.6cm) of organic matter. The long branches need strong support. Guide the young shoots to where you want them to grow. To create a bushy plant, pinch the growing tips of the branches. Prune in early spring or fall to control size and thin the vines. This is an excellent shade plant for a patio or terrace. It is lovely draped over the top of a wall or left as a ground cover to cascade down a slope.

Cape Honeysuckle

Tecomaria capensis (Bignoniaceae)

Native to South Africa, cape honeysuckle is a vigorous, evergreen, twining vine that is hardy in Zones 9 and 10. It grows 8 to 10 feet (2.4–3m) long. Shiny, dark green, oval leaflets, borne five to nine on a stem, give this vine a delicate, lacy appearance. The vibrant red-orange blooms put on a show in late summer through autumn. The funnel-shaped blooms are 2 inches (5.1cm) long, with prominent stamens. Unsupported, cape honeysuckle

CHILEAN JASMINE

makes a good ground cover, easily grown on hot dry slopes. It is effective trained as an espalier or grown on a trellis, forming a dense screen. Slender branches bear shiny, dark green leaves.

Grow it in full sun in any well-drained soil. Keep the plant evenly moist until it is established; after that, it can tolerate some drought. Cape honeysuckle is fairly rugged and is tolerant of windy conditions. It will grow in full shade, but there it will be less floriferous. A light frost will nip the plant, but it will survive. Prune as necessary to control the shape and keep the plant under control. In late autumn or winter cut back the stems to stimulate new flowering wood. 'Aurea' is a yellow-flowered variety that is less vigorous and less hardy.

Chilean Jasmine

Mandevilla laxa (Apocynaceae)

Contrary to its name, the twining vine known as Chilean jasmine is native to Bolivia and northern Argentina. It is a quick-growing, deciduous vine that can reach 20 feet (6.1m) and is hardy in Zones 8 to 10. The leaves, up to 3 inches (7.6cm) long, are borne on long stems. It is grown mainly for the funnel-shaped flowers that open to a delicate white starburst up to 2 inches (5.1cm) across. Highly fragrant, the flowers bloom all summer.

Plant in full sun in rich, humusy, moist soil that has been amended with plenty of organic matter. Keep the soil evenly moist throughout the flowering season. Cut back on water as the plant stops blooming. In early spring, feed by mulching with well-rotted manure. To keep the lush growth of foliage, occasionally pinch back the growing tips. This vine rarely needs a severe pruning, unless it has been damaged by frost. Unlike mandevilla, Chilean jasmine is not suited to pot culture; it does not like having its roots restricted or confined. It is the perfect vine for growing up open trellises, arbors, and treillage.

Chinese Jasmine

Jasminum polyanthum (Oleaceae)

The vigorous Chinese jasmine grows to 20 feet (6.1m). It is hardy in Zones 8 to 10. The finely textured leaflets distinguish this from other jasmines. The starlike blooms perfume the air from February into summer. The flowers, borne in dense clusters on side branches, are white with rosy pink on the outside. Chinese jasmine makes a great ground cover in partial shade, is recommended for container culture, and will grow in small spaces when trained on a trellis. Prune after it finishes flowering in autumn to keep the plant under control and prevent tangling. See Jasmine (page 102) for cultivation tips.

Chinese Trumpet Creeper

Campsis grandiflora (Bignoniaceae)

Hardy in Zones 7 and 8, Chinese trumpet creeper is more restrained in its growth than trumpet creeper vine, making it suitable for smaller gardens. It is magnificent in midsummer with its large, scarlet blooms. See Trumpet Creeper (page 110) for cultivation tips.

CHINESE WISTERIA

Chinese Wisteria

Wisteria sinensis (Fabaceae)

Chinese wisteria is outstanding for its showy blooms. All the blue-violet flowers in the 6- to 12-inch (15.2–30.5cm) long panicles open at once, blooming just before the leaves open. Leaflets are 2 to 3 inches (5.1–7.6cm) long in groups of seven to thirteen. 'Alba' has pure white, fragrant flowers. 'Purpurea' bears the popular violet blooms. 'Plena' is a double-flowered variety. *Wisteria × formosa* is a hybrid of Japanese and Chinese wisteria. See Wisteria (page 114) for cultivation tips.

CLEMATIS

Clematis spp. (Ranunculaceae)

Regal vines in form and flower, clematis are often called "queen of climbers." Queen during the day, they are equally majestic in the garden in early evening. There are evergreen and deciduous species of this twining vine. With more than one hundred named cultivars, the flowers come in a variety of sizes, shapes, and colors, ranging from large open saucers to dainty bells in hues of cerise, pink, mauve, purple, lavender, blue, yellow, and white. Clematis are surprisingly long-lasting as cut flowers. The seedpods, which follow the flowers, are highly ornamental, both on the vines and in dried-flower arrangements. Clematis are well-mannered vines, with twisting, slender stems. Depending on the variety, they are hardy from Zones 4 to 10.

Clematis prefer slightly alkaline, rich, moist, well-drained, well-worked soil. They are particular, growing best where the vines get full sun, while the roots are cool and shaded. Dig a deep hole, at least twice as deep as the roots. Amend the soil with plenty of organic matter. Check the pH and adjust if necessary to about 7.0, adding lime to acid soil, bone meal to very alkaline soil. Place half of the amended soil back in the hole. Place the support for the clematis before you plant the vine. Plant the crown 2 to 3 inches (5.2 to 7.5cm) deep and cover with soil. Mulch well with organic material. Clematis are shallow rooted; do not cultivate around the plant or allow root competition from nearby plants. Fertilize once during the growing season with a balanced fertilizer. Water regularly.

Gently tie the fragile stems to a support. Clematis do not need strong support; they will grow happily on a trellis. Pruning depends on when the plant blooms. After flowering, cut back the current season's wood on those clematis that bloom in early summer to fall. If you wait until spring, cut it back when the buds swell. Prune the plant back to 6 to 12 inches (15.2–30.5cm) for bushy new growth, with maximum new wood for the new flowers. Clematis that bloom in midspring flower on one-year-old wood; prune them lightly after they flower, remove seedpods, and thin slightly.

'JACKMANII SUPERBA' CLEMATIS

'VILLE DE LYON' CLEMATIS

Choose from the hundreds of varieties—you will likely have many favorites. 'Ville de Lyon' has 5-inch, (12.7cm) velvety carmine flowers on 10- to 12-foot (3–3.7m) vines. 'Nelly Moser' is a classic, with pale pink petals and a central stripe of deep pink; the huge, 7- to 9-inch (17.8–22.9cm) flowers bloom profusely in May and June, and often repeat in September. Include white-flowering varieties in your collection such as 'Henryi' or the luscious double 'Duchess of Edinburgh', and the queen continues her reign throughout the day into the night, and from late spring through autumn. See also Evergreen Clematis (page 97), Jackman Clematis (page 100), Scarlet Clematis (page 108), and Sweet Autumn Clematis (page 110).

CLIMBING HYDRANGEA

Climbing Hydrangea

Hydrangea petiolaris (Saxifragaceae)

Climbing hydrangea is a deciduous, flowering vine with the potential to grow to 50 feet (15.2m) or more, hardy in Zones 5 to 9. It is not a vine for those who are faint of heart; almost a bigger-than-life vine, it needs to be grown where its size is in scale to its surroundings. It is not rampant, however, but slow to get established; after that it turns into a vigorous climber. Climbing hydrangea has aerial rootlets that anchor it firmly, but unless its support is firmly in the ground, it can topple. In spring, the vine leafs out with attractive, finely toothed, heart-shaped leaves. Late in spring, it is resplendent with lacy white-cap flower clusters 6 to 8 inches (15.2–20.3cm) across, held away from the foliage on long stems. In autumn the leaves drop to reveal the handsome shedding red bark that adds interest to the winter garden.

Grow climbing hydrangea in partial shade to full sun. It prefers deep, moist, well-drained, fertile loam. Amend the soil with plenty of organic matter before planting. It is best grown against an indestructible surface; the rootlets can destroy masonry and wood structures. It is handsome when it climbs up a large, established tree. Without support, it is still impressive as a rambling, creeping vine. Prune to thin and keep in shape as needed. If flower production decreases, give the vine a severe rejuvenative pruning in winter or early spring.

CLIMBING ROSE

Rosa spp. (Rosaceae)

Climbing roses, despite their name, are not true climbers. They are simply rose varieties with particularly long canes (stems) that must be trained and secured to an upright. Unsupported, the canes sprawl, forming a somewhat mounded shrub that can be attractive in an informal landscape. Climbing roses add grace and elegance to any garden. Depending on how they are trained, the look can be formal or informal. Trained over an arch, climbing roses add a romantic feel to the garden; trained up posts and then along rope or chain draped between posts, these roses can create a formal border to a garden. A rose arbor is a beautiful sight to behold. Roses are hardy in Zones 5 to 10, depending on the variety. The canes can grow anywhere from 10 to 50 feet (3–15.2m) in length, also depending on the variety.

Roses need full sun for best flower production. Choose a spot with good air circulation. Plant in rich, well-drained loam to which plenty of organic matter has been added. Allow ample space between plants. Roses are shallow-rooted plants and heavy feeders, so do not disturb the roots by growing other plants at their base. Mulch well around the rose, and keep it well watered throughout the growing season. Feed in spring when the buds break, again when they begin to bloom, and once again a month later. Pruning needs vary somewhat according to the type of rose. In general, prune in spring before the leaf buds break, to eliminate any dead wood. Renew the plants by cutting back one or more of the oldest canes. Cut off spent blooms to encourage reblooming and to give the plant a tidier, more robust look.

Three types of roses are grouped together under the general category of climbing rose: large-flowered climbers, climbing sports, and ramblers. Large-flowered climbers are cold hardy (to -18 degrees F [-27.8°C]), and are best suited to cold winter areas. They are characterized by stout, stiff canes that grow from 8 to 15 feet (2.4–4.6m) tall. The flowers range from 2 to 6 inches (5.1–15.2cm) across, appearing as a big burst of bloom in late spring, and they bloom throughout the growing season. Flowers are formed on the 6- to 12-inch (15.2–30.5cm) laterals of two- and three-year-old canes. In early spring, cut the laterals back to 3 to 6 inches (7.6–15.2cm), removing all but three or four buds. Some choice varieties include medium pink 'Blossomtime'; fragrant, coral pink 'Coral Dawn'; highly scented 'Dr. J.H. Nicolas'; pale pink, edged in deep pink 'Handel'; 'Joseph's Coat', with showy, deep golden yellow blooms suffused with orange and red, changing color as they mature; and the favorite yellow 'Golden Showers'.

LADY BANKS ROSE

'CLIMBING CECILE BRUNNER' ROSE

Climbing sports come from bush roses that threw out an exceptionally long cane. The canes are vegetatively propagated, resulting in long-caned plants with the same flowers as many favorite garden roses. An easy way to tell if a rose is a climbing sport is that it will have "climbing" as the first word of its name. Some very popular roses have climbing sports. It can be fun to pair a climbing and a bush form of the same rose together. The colors available in climbing rose plants range through all the expected hues, as evidenced by small, pink-flowered 'Climbing Cecile Brunner'; large, bold pink-flowered 'Climbing Charlotte Armstrong'; deep red 'Climbing Chrysler Imperial'; deep pink 'Climbing First Prize'; orange-flowered 'Climbing Mrs. Sam McGrady'; the favorite multitoned yellow 'Climbing Peace'; and white 'Climbing Iceberg'.

Once tied to the support, the biggest climbing roses should be left to grow without pruning until they get as tall as you want them. Then, the plants should be bent to grow over a fence or trellis. The horizontal branches will produce the most and biggest roses. Without pruning, they will continue to bloom for several years. To encourage larger blooms, remove lateral branches and cut the flowering shoots back to 3 or 4 inches (7.6–10.2cm) in early spring.

Ramblers are long-caned roses that can grow longer than 20 feet (6.1m). The canes are supple, allowing them to be trained easily in arches. Most, with protection, are hardy to -10 degrees F (-23.3°C). The flowers are produced on one-year-old canes. Prune the roses early each spring to remove old wood, allowing space for new flowering canes. With support, ramblers are lovely covering tall fences. Left on their own, they can be exquisite, colorful (but thorny) ground covers. *Rosa banksiae*, Lady Banks rose, bears a profusion of pale yellow flowers; 'Evangeline' has single pink blooms; 'Chevy Chase' has small red flowers. Some of these roses can be extremely long-lived, given the right conditions. Planted in 1906, 'Dorothy Perkins' with its lovely pink flowers is still blooming on a rose arbor at Planting Fields Arboretum in Oyster Bay, New York.

Coral Vine

Antigonon leptopus (Polygonaceae)

A native of Mexico, coral vine is widely grown in the hot regions of the United States, particularly in the South, Southwest, and California. It goes by many names: rosa de montaña, mountain rose, corallita, queen's wreath, and Confederate vine. A deciduous, flowering vine that climbs by tendrils, it bears deep rose, pink or, rarely, white flowers in long trailing sprays from midsummer into fall. As long as the weather stays warm, the flowers will last on the vine. The blooms are long-lasting as cut flowers. Coral vine has a graceful habit with branches that cascade and curl back on themselves, making it appear to be covered in bloom. The leaves are attractive, with a distinctive, folded heart shape, and bright spring-green color. It is hardy in Zones 8 to 10.

Coral vine needs full sun and very well-drained soil; it thrives in locations that could bake other plants. Grow it in poor soil and it will reward you by growing from 20 to 40 feet (6.1–12.2m) by the end of the summer. It climbs by tendrils located at the ends of the flowering branches. However, these branches do not appear right away, so attach the young vine to a strong support to promote vertical growth. It works well on an arbor, or secured to the wall of a house. Trained on a fence, it provides an effective screen during the growing season. Let it grow along the ground, and it will prove itself to be a tough ground cover, rapidly covering bare areas.

A low-maintenance plant, coral vine thrives with little attention, and is pest- and disease-resistant. Do not fertilize, unless you want a profusion of leaves and few flowers. It is drought-tolerant, but appreciates regular, deep watering in summer. During periods of prolonged drought, it may die back to the ground in midsummer. The thick, tuberous roots are winter hardy, and it will quickly send up new stems in the spring. Minor frost may cause some dieback, but as long as the roots do not freeze, the vine will rejuvenate. Thin and shape by pruning in autumn. After the flowers fade, you can cut the vine back to the base in autumn. Mulch the roots well if the temperature threatens to go below 25 degrees F (-1.1°C).

CREEPING FIG

Creeping Fig

Ficus pumila (Moraceae)

An evergreen vine with a vigor that belies its diminutive size, creeping fig is native to eastern Asia. Hardy in Zones 9 and 10, it is often grown as a greenhouse plant elsewhere. Its small, rootlike hold-fasts can adhere this

Creeping fig thrives in partial shade in rich, moist soil. Tie the plant to a support until the hold-fasts develop. Mist the branches regularly to encourage hold-fast growth and lush foliage. Pinch the growing tips to encourage branching. Cut back and thin the stems as needed to keep the plant within bounds, reduce overall mass, and discourage mature growth. Creeping fig is beautiful climbing up a wall (even glass bricks), and can be trained on a trellis to form an attractive screen. Indoors, it is equally effective in a hanging basket or in a container near a sunny window.

'Minima' has smaller and daintier leaves than the species. 'Quercifolia' has lobed leaves that look just like tiny oak leaves. 'Variegata' adds dimension wherever it grows with its green and white variegated leaves.

Cross Vine

Bignonia capreolata (Bignoniaceae)

Cross vine, native to Maryland, is a strong, evergreen vine hardy to Zone 7. The compound green leaves turn a lovely reddish-green in fall and persist through winter, adding to the otherwise short season of color for this easy-to-grow plant. The 2-inch (5.1cm) long, trumpet-shaped, red-orange flowers bloom in small clusters in May and June. The flared portion of the flowers is a sunny yellow-orange. It is not until you look very closely at cross vine that the reason for its name is revealed. Cut the end of the stem, and the pattern in the tissue forms a cross. This semihardy climber can grow to 50 feet (15.2m); the branching terminal tendrils have adhesive disks.

Plant cross vine in full sun, and it will thrive in a variety of settings. It is tolerant of wind, humidity, dryness, heat, and cold; however, it will succumb in extended freezing weather. Its method of climbing will not harm structures, so it is ideal for training to grow up the wall of a house, garage, barn, or a solid fence. The best time to prune cross vine is in early spring. Prune out any dead wood or weak branches. Give it an all-over pruning back of several feet to encourage vigorous, new, flowering growth.

tough little vine to stone, wood, or even glass. It is beautiful to see it covering a wall, with wiry branching stems that form a delicate tracery accented by heart-shaped, deeply veined leaves. Like ivy, its juvenile and mature forms are widely different. The juvenile form is generally preferred, with small, 1-inch (2.5cm) leaves borne on the clinging stems that can form a tight mat. The mature form bears much larger, somewhat leathery, coarse foliage that tends to hang away from the mass of immature stems. Prune out mature stems, if you like, to keep the plant in the desired form.

Dutchman's Pipe

Aristolochia durior (Aristolochiaceae)

Dutchman's pipe, a deciduous, American native, woody vine, can quickly grow to 30 feet (9.1m) or more, after a slow start. It grows wild from Pennsylvania to Georgia and Kansas, and is hardy to Zone 4. It is the perfect twining vine to provide cooling summer shade, yet it lets the sun through in winter. Dutchman's pipe rapidly covers any offending view with lovely, large (6 to 14 inches [15.2–35.6cm]), glossy green, overlapping leaves. With its rampant growth, it is considered by some a northern rival to kudzu. It needs very strong support; a large trellis or lattice is ideal. The flowers, often hidden under the leaves, are 1½ to 3 inches (3.8–7.6cm) wide, each resembling a calabash pipe (broadly tubular), and are rather malodorous.

Dutchman's pipe is weedlike. It will grow in full sun to partial shade, in any soil or moisture. For best results, it prefers even moisture. In areas with cold winters, protect the first-year plant once the weather gets cold with a layer of mulch. Once it is established, let it go on its own. Pruning is necessary only to keep the vine within bounds. Head back and thin the plant in spring or summer. In mild climates, it can remain evergreen.

Two related species, *Aristolochia elegans* (calico flower) and *A. grandiflora* (pelican flower), are suited for outdoor culture in California and southern Florida, hardy only in Zone 10. In other areas they are good greenhouse plants.

English Ivy

Hedera helix (Araliaceae)

This is the vine that most people refer to as "ivy." It is a tough plant whose versatility in the landscape has been demonstrated for centuries. Whether grown as a formal ground cover, planted on a hillside for erosion control, trained on a fence to resemble an evergreen hedge, or allowed to climb its way up the walls of an edifice, the aerial roots hold the ivy well in place. English ivy is easily kept in bounds by judicious pruning. Never let it grow where you don't want it. The tenacious roots are likely to rip

'GOLDHEART' ENGLISH IVY

the paint off a building, and pull off pieces of brick and mortar when you try to pull down an established patch of ivy. The leaves are handsome, glossy, and leathery green, 2 to 4 inches (5–10cm) long with lighter green veins.

English ivy will grow in full sun to partial shade; it is prized as a shade-loving ground cover. In hot, dry climates, and snowy winter areas, it needs partial shade to protect the leaves. It prefers neutral to slightly alkaline, well-drained, moist soil, although it will grow almost anywhere. To promote rooting and quick growth, add organic matter to the soil and keep the soil evenly moist, watering only in the morning. To grow ivy as a ground cover, allow 12 to 18 inches (30.5–45.7cm) between plants.

English ivy can be pruned regularly to keep it in shape and control its mass. When it is grown as a ground cover, perhaps the easiest way to prune it and encourage new growth is to mow it in early spring. It may look pitiful for a week or two, but new leaves appear quickly to replace those removed. English ivy lends itself for use in topiary, and trains well to follow forms, whether formal or whimsical. Prune it as necessary when it is in training.

More than a hundred varieties have been developed, each unique in its own way. Some of the best known are yellow-variegated 'Aureo-variegata'; very hardy 'Baltica', with white veins; somewhat drought-tolerant 'Bulgaria'; '238th Street', a New York City find with heart-shaped leaves; five-to-seven-lobed 'Digitata'; 'Fluffy Ruffles', with small leaves with wavy edges; and 'Goldheart', with yellow markings at the center of the leaves.

Evergreen Clematis

Clematis armandii (Ranunculaceae)

The most tender of its genus, evergreen clematis is hardy only in Zones 8 to 10 and can grow to 25 feet (7.6m). The shiny, dark green foliage that stays on the vine year-round makes this a good background plant even when it is not in bloom. Fragrant white flowers, 1 to 2½ inches (2.5–6.4cm) across, bloom in early spring, followed by handsome, plump seedpods in summer. It is beautiful planted along a fence, draped along the top of eaves, trained up a tall, bare tree trunk, or covering a strong arbor. Prune after it blooms; it flowers on old wood. 'Apple Blossom' has pale pink flowers. See Clematis (page 89) for cultivation tips.

Five-Leaf Akebia

Akebia quinata (Lardizabalaceae)

Native to Japan, China, and Korea, this semievergreen, twining climber grows quickly to 30 feet (9m). Five-leaf akebia is hardy to Zone 4, and is evergreen in the warmer end of its range, deciduous in the colder areas. The compound leaves are composed of five leaflets, as the name implies, which give a graceful look to this vine. In spring, spicy-scented male and female flowers open in clusters. The male flowers are a rosy, purplish-brown, while the females are a darker, purplish, violet-brown. Rarely does the vine fruit without hand pollination; then, it produces cloyingly sweet, seedy, purple fruit in late summer to fall. This is a beautiful vine to create light shade when grown on a trellis. It has a delicate appearance and is a good choice for planting on a fence.

Plant five-leaf akebia in a warm, sunny spot in light, well-drained, humusy soil that is neutral to slightly acidic. Although it will grow in shade, it will not tolerate heavy or alkaline soils. Head it back with hard pruning each year, or it will grow completely out of control, especially in warm areas where it does not naturally die back in winter. It is a tough vine, and can bounce back quickly, even when cut right to the ground.

Giant Burmese Honeysuckle

Lonicera hildebrandiana (Caprifoliaceae)

An evergreen vine, giant Burmese honeysuckle is the largest of the honeysuckles, with twining, ropelike branches that can reach 40 to 80 feet (12.2–24.4m). It is hardy in Zones 9 and 10. The attractive dark green, shiny, 4- to 6-inch (10.2–15.2cm) leaves are a lovely contrast to the

FIVE-LEAF AKEBIA

slender, 7-inch (17.8cm), tubular flowers. The blooms of the giant Burmese Honeysuckle open in summer; they are creamy white fading to varying shades of yellow to gold, and then drop off the vine. Dark green, berrylike fruit follow in autumn.

Giant Burmese honeysuckle cannot tolerate temperatures below 32 degrees F (0°C) for any length of time. A prodigious vine, it requires lots of room and very sturdy support. It is well suited to being draped across the tops of high walls. Train it as an espalier against a fence, or put its rampant habit to good use as a ground cover on a slope. In coastal areas grow it in full sun, and in hotter areas, plant it in partial shade. See Honeysuckle (below) for cultivation tips.

Guinea Gold Vine

Hibbertia scandens (Dilleniaceae)

An Australian native, this twining, evergreen, flowering vine (also known as gold guinea plant or button flower) is hardy in Zone 10, well suited for the frost-free areas of the deep South and California. Guinea gold vine grows to 15 feet (4.6m), with slender, reddish-brown stems, creating a tall, shrubby vine. Without support, it becomes a dense ground cover. The attractive, dark green, glossy leaves have light, hairy undersides. Golden yellow, open, five-petaled flowers are 2 to 3 inches (5.1–7.6cm) across, resembling wild roses with their prominent yellow stamens. The lightly musk-scented blooms grace the vine from late spring until early fall.

Guinea gold vine grows best in moist, well-drained soil. Although it likes sun, protect it from hot, reflected sunlight and scalding winds. Leaves are easily killed by cold, but after a light frost the plant will send out new foliage. This plant grows quickly, and needs pruning to keep it within bounds. Prune to remove unwanted branches and reduce top growth in early spring before it flowers, or in autumn after it finishes blooming. Fertilize in early spring. This is a great vine for growing on a fence, by an entranceway, as a living screen, on an arbor, or even in a large container. It is a striking plant that can manage well in relatively small spaces.

Herald's Trumpet

Beaumontia grandiflora (Apocynaceae)

A tender, evergreen vine, herald's trumpet (also called Easter lily vine) is a real showstopper when it blooms in spring and summer with fragrant white flowers that resemble trumpets of lily. Upon closer examination, the 5-inch (12.7cm) flowers, borne in clusters at the ends of the branches, are lightly tipped in pink, with green veins at the throat. The large, glossy, 6- to 9-inch (12.2–22.9cm) leaves are handsome by themselves, giving a tropical look to this Himalayan native. Hardy to Zone 10, herald's trumpet will grow 15 to 30 feet (4.6–9.1m), with a twining, arching form. It is a perfect accent in a grand garden, planted where it can get a lot of attention. It makes a good screen, easily covering a fence or twining up a column.

Herald's trumpet needs full sun and rich, well-drained soil that has been amended with plenty of organic matter such as compost or well-rotted manure. Give the roots and the vine itself ample room to spread out. It thrives in heat and high humidity, but languishes in cold and dry climates. In early spring, before flowering, water well and fertilize; you will be rewarded with magnificent blooms and luxuriant foliage. The vine is heavy and needs sturdy support. Start to train the vine early on and it will respond well. Prune in autumn, thinning out older branches to reduce the overall mass of the vine, and to encourage production of lateral flowering shoots. It flowers on old wood, so be careful when pruning to leave enough one- to three-year-old wood to bear the next year's flowers.

HONEYSUCKLE

Lonicera spp. (Caprifoliaceae)

There are more than 150 species of honeysuckle, though only a few are readily available and desirable in cultivation. Honeysuckles are twining vines with showy, sometimes fragrant flowers that attract hummingbirds. Other birds are attracted to the berries. They can grow almost anywhere; unimpeded, they can be rampant. In cultivation that can be a good thing, as a vine can quickly cover a fence or hide an ugly garage. In the wild, though, honeysuckle (especially the Japanese variety) can choke out other plants, so keep the plants under control. See also Giant Burmese Honeysuckle (page 98), Japanese Honeysuckle (page 101), and Trumpet Honeysuckle (page 111).

I V Y

Hedera spp. (Araliaceae)

Ivies are among the world's foremost evergreen vines. Traditionally used as ground covers, ivies will happily grow vertically when given support for their aerial roots. The leaves are triangularly heart-shaped.

Ivies have two forms, juvenile and mature. Most commonly seen is the juvenile form, with its vining habit. If a vine is not pruned as it ages, it will form mature branches with an upright habit. Often the leaves are larger, and more rounded; at first glance it looks like a small shrub has taken hold in the middle of a bed of ivy. Clusters of small, white, starry flowers appear, followed by green to blackish berries. Cut a mature stem of ivy, root and plant it, and it will grow into an upright shrub. Regular pruning will keep a vine in the juvenile form. Sometimes it is fun to leave one mature stem, just to pique the interest of visitors to your garden. See English Ivy (page 96) for cultivation tips. See also Algerian Ivy (page 83).

Jackman Clematis

Clematis jackmanii (Ranunculaceae)

Jackman clematis was the first large-flowered hybrid developed, and it is still a favorite. The abundant purple blossoms, 4 to 6 inches (10.2–15.2cm) in diameter, flower from July to October on slender, twisting stems. It can grow 12 to 15 feet (3.7–4.6m) tall. It is lovely trained on an arbor with pink or white roses. Jackman clematis dies down to the ground in cold winter areas, and grows again each spring. Cultivars arising from this hybrid include the lovely pink 'Comtesse de Bouchard',

HERALD'S TRUMPET

JAPANESE HONEYSUCKLE

brilliant pink 'Rubra', and scarlet-purple 'Mme. Edouard Andre'. See Clematis (page 89) for cultivation tips.

Japanese Honeysuckle

Lonicera japonica (Caprifoliaceae)

Japanese honeysuckle was imported into America from Japan around the turn of the century. It is often described as an evergreen twining vine that climbs or covers the ground, self-rooting as it goes. The slightly hairy vine can easily grow to 30 feet (9.1m) in length. The 2- to 3-inch (5.1–7.6cm) leaves, narrowly heart-shaped, are deep green, often downy below, less commonly downy above. The flowers appear in May and continue to bloom sporadically through late summer.

There is nothing quite like the sweet scent of Japanese honeysuckle. It is hardy in Zones 4 to 10. Gardeners have been discouraged in the last decade from planting it. As you drive around the countryside in summer, you can smell its sweet scent wafting from gardens and from woodlands where it has escaped and naturalized. In warm areas it is evergreen, in colder climates semievergreen. The flower buds are tinged purple, open white, and turn pale yellow as they mature. The flowers, borne in pairs at the bases of leaves, look like thin tubes with curled-back lips and prominent stamens. You probably sucked on the sweet nectar as a child (it still tastes as good as it did back then).

Considered a weed by many, it will grow in inhospitable places scorned by other plants. In sun or shade, sandy or poorly drained soil, Japanese honeysuckle will thrive. It spreads rapidly as branches that touch the ground quickly root. To keep it in bounds, prune it severely and as often as needed. It is good as a ground cover for erosion control, but it is charming trained on a trellis. Several choice varieties are not as rampant as the species. 'Purpurea', purple honeysuckle (sometimes referred to as 'Chinensis'), has flowers that are tinged reddish-purple and leaves fringed in purple. 'Halliana', or Hall's honeysuckle, bears white flowers and green leaves. 'Gold Net' honeysuckle is distinctive for its yellow variegated leaves; it is more tender than other varieties. See Honeysuckle (page 99) for cultivation tips.

Japanese Wisteria

Wisteria floribunda (Fabaceae)

The panicles of flowers of Japanese wisteria open from top to bottom. Flower clusters range in length from 8 to 48 inches (20.3cm–1.2m), in shades of white, pink, and violet. It has thirteen to nineteen 1- to 2-inch (2.5–5.1cm) leaflets that comprise the compound leaf. There are more than forty recognized varieties. 'Alba' bears white flowers in 18- to 24-inch (45.7–61cm) panicles. 'Issai' has blue-violet flowers in 12-inch (30.5cm) clusters. 'Violacea Plena' has lovely double purple flowers. 'Rosea' bears fragrant pink blooms. 'Macrobotrys' is magnificent with purple-blue flowers on three-foot (91cm)-long panicles. 'Longissima' has the longest flower cluster—up to 4 feet (1.2m). See Wisteria (page 114) for cultivation tips.

JASMINE

Jasminum spp. (Oleaceae)

True jasmines are evergreen, fragrant flowering vines, hardy only in Zones 8 to 10, depending on the type. In colder areas, they make good houseplants, blooming in winter. The evergreen, compound foliage is a handsome backdrop to the long-lasting flowers. The twining stems need a secure fence or post to climb. Often the stems will fall off; guide wires help. They are effective draped over a wall, and without support make lovely ground covers.

Plant jasmine in full sun in light, well-drained loam. If the plant must be shaded, provide afternoon rather than morning shade, or bloom quantity will be adversely affected. Water regularly, and mulch well to keep the soil lightly moist. Fertilize in early spring or summer. Pinch the growing tips to increase flowering and encourage a bushy habit. Jasmine can be propagated from tip cuttings in summer or autumn. To keep the vine in control, head it back in late autumn.

JAPANESE WISTERIA

Jasmines are excellent for container culture, outdoors or in. Indoors, grow jasmine in bright light, with several hours of full sun a day. It prefers 60-degree-F (15.6°C) nights and 80-degree-F (26.7°C) days. Keep plant lightly moist in spring and summer. Feed every two weeks. In fall and winter, allow the soil to dry out a bit between waterings. During that period, do not fertilize. In the spring, prune the stems back and repot the plant, using an all-purpose potting mix. See also Angel Wing Jasmine (page 83), Arabian Jasmine (page 84), and Chinese Jasmine (page 88).

KOLOMIKTA VINE

Kolomikta Vine

Actinidia kolomikta (Actinidiaceae)

Native to eastern Asia, this decorative, twining vine, a relative of the kiwi, is grown for its handsome variegated foliage. Like the other actinidias, kolomikta is a dioecious vine, with separate male and female plants. Hardy to Zone 4, it can grow to 15 feet (4.6m). Only the male of this species is cultivated; when young, the leaves have pink, red, white, and cream variegations. The ¾-inch (1.9cm) white flowers in spring are pretty, but they are a secondary attraction. Grown on an arbor or trellis, this vine will cast a nice area of cooling shade.

Plant in partial shade to avoid the scalding midday sun, especially in warmer areas. Grow in rich, humusy, well-drained, moist soil. Keep the plant evenly moist. In early spring or fall, prune as necessary to remove dead wood and to train the vine.

Madagascar Jasmine

Stephanotis floribunda (Asclepiadaceae)

Native to Madagascar, this woody, evergreen climber (also called floradora or wax-flower) is hardy in Zones 9 and 10. A twining vine, it can grow to 15 feet (4.6m). It is grown outdoors in California and Florida; in the rest of the country it may be cultivated as a greenhouse or houseplant. Prized for its white, waxy, funnel-shaped flowers, Madagascar jasmine is used in the floral trade in bridal bouquets and floral arrangements. Thick, dark green, leathery leaves grow to 4 inches (10.2cm) long, making a perfect background for the highly fragrant, white summer blooms.

Madagasar jasmine, like clematis, grows best when its roots are shaded. The foliage does well in partial shade—midday sun can burn the leaves. Plant Madagascar jasmine in rich, well-drained soil, and keep the plant lightly moist. Pruning, best done in autumn, is rarely needed, except to train the plant or cut out dead wood. Madagascar jasmine is exquisite climbing a small trellis. Weave it through a lattice to create the altar for a special June wedding.

'Madame Galen' Trumpet Creeper

Campsis × tagliabuana 'Madame Galen' (Bignoniaceae)

A somewhat restrained trumpet creeper, 'Madame Galen' is a hybrid of two species (*Campsis radicans* and *C. grandiflora*), growing 25 to 30 feet (7.6–9.1m) high. It is hardy from Zones 4 to 8. Gorgeous salmon-red flowers are borne in loose clusters. See Trumpet Creeper (page 110) for cultivation tips.

Mandevilla

Mandevilla splendens (Apocynaceae)

Native to southeastern Brazil, the twining mandevilla vine is hardy in Zone 10. Given suitable conditions it will grow to 20 feet (6.1m). Shiny, ribbed, evergreen leaves, up to 6 inches (15.2cm) long and 3 inches (7.6cm) wide, give a tropical look to mandevilla even when it is not in bloom. The beautiful, bright pink flowers with a flared trumpet shape are borne in abundance from spring to autumn.

Plant this vine in full sun in rich, humusy, moist soil that has been amended with plenty of organic matter. Keep the soil evenly moist throughout the flowering season. Cut back on water as the plant stops blooming. In early spring, feed by mulching with well-rotted manure. To keep the lush growth of foliage, occasionally pinch back the growing tips. This vine rarely needs a severe pruning, unless it has been damaged by frost. It is a very popular vine (especially in California), magnificent trained up a trellis, post, arch, arbor, or ramada. It makes an excellent container plant, so its popularity is growing in areas with severe winters, where it can either be treated as a lovely annual that dies when the weather gets cold, or brought indoors and enjoyed as a houseplant through the colder months. *Mandevilla × amabilis* 'Alice du Pont' is a choice cultivar with lovely salmon-pink flowers.

Moonseed

Menispermum canadense (Menispermaceae)

Moonseed is another hardy, twining vine that is considered a weed by some gardeners. It can spread by underground stems, popping up where you least expect it. That habit makes it a choice vine for covering barren slopes in short order. Hardy to Zone 3, the vine grows to 12 feet (3.7m). It gets its name from its crescent-shaped seeds. The abundant, dark green, glossy leaves grow 4 to 8 inches (10.2–20.3cm) long and 4 to 5 inches (10.2–12.7cm) across, with three to seven lobes, creating a luxuriant effect. It is dioecious. Inconspicuous yellowish-white flowers bloom from late spring to late summer. The female vines bear black, grapelike fruit.

Plant in partial shade in well-drained, moist soil. It will grow in full sun provided it receives ample water, but will die in a hot, dry climate. The stems die back after the first frost, and reemerge in spring. It is an excellent plant in a wildlife habitat or semiboggy woodland where its vigorous growth may be welcomed rather than scorned. In the garden, plant it against a shaded wall or on a light lattice. Pruning is usually not necessary.

Night-Blooming Cereus

Hylocereus undatus (Cactaceae)

Night-blooming cereus is not usually included with vines and climbers. Yet to my mind, if climbing roses are given a place, so should at least one of the so-called "clambering" cacti. A number of different cacti and succulents, all related, are commonly called "night-blooming cereus," including *Nyctocereus, Lemaireocereus, Selenicereus,* and *Cereus.* I selected this one to represent the group as it is the most outstanding, as evidenced by its other common name: queen of the night. It grows wild in much of South America, but its true origins are unknown. Hardy to Zone 10, it is grown indoors in areas without hard frosts. Slow-growing, it can clamber on the ground, and even climb rugged palm trees by means of the aerial roots that dangle from the stem. Hylocereus has thick, succulent stems with three

NIGHT-BLOOMING CEREUS

tantalizingly slowly, petal by petal. It takes several hours until they are fully opened. The flowers can measure up to 12 inches (30.5cm) across. The narrow outer petals, which flush pink as the flower opens, are recurved as if to better show off the layers of broad, pure white inner petals. The inner petals surround the prominent, creamy-yellow stamens like a hoop petticoat. Viewed from slightly off center, the long pistil looks like a sea cucumber with waving tentacles. Once fully opened, the flower emits a hauntingly sweet aroma, quite unlike any other I've smelled, which in the wild would attract the bats, hylocereus' pollinators. The flowers last only until the first hint of daylight, when they collapse like deflated balloons.

This cactus is obviously not for every household. In California it will grow outdoors in a sunny location in very well-drained soil to which plenty of organic matter has been added. It is a good pot plant, best grown in a mixture that is coarse and fertile, with ample sand or vermiculite so that it is very free-draining. It likes to be fairly pot-bound. Allow the lower portion of the stem and the top of the uppermost roots to show at the surface of the soil. When the plant is young, repot it every two to three years. As it gets older, or once it has been planted in a 10-inch (25.4cm) or larger pot, it can wait longer between repottings. Grow it on a sunny window in a cool room from fall to spring. In summer, set it in a partially shaded spot outdoors. Soak the soil thoroughly, then let it dry almost completely before resoaking. In summer, water about once a week; in winter there should be longer intervals between waterings. If pot-bound, fertilize with liquid houseplant fertilizer once a month from spring to early fall. Stems tend to be weak or trailing and may need support, whether the plant is grown indoors or out.

prominent ribs. It is not a plant that is grown for its foliage—if truth be told, it is an awkward-looking, gangly cactus.

The flowers, which bloom only one night a year, are the reason you put up with this plant for the other 364 days. Be patient, as it is not until the cactus is several years old that it will flower, usually in mid- to late summer. One or more flower buds form along the stem. When the buds are 1 to 2 inches (2.5–5.1cm) long, keep a watchful eye out. One night (often when there is a full moon), about eight or nine o'clock, the buds begin to open,

Oriental Bittersweet

Celastrus orbiculatus (Celastraceae)

Hardy in Zones 5 to 9, Oriental bittersweet is a very vigorous vine that can spread to 40 feet (12.2m). It is characterized by its round leaves and lateral fruiting branches. It is well suited for quickly covering large areas. See Bittersweet (page 84) for cultivation tips.

PASSIONFLOWER

PASSIONFLOWER

Passiflora spp. (Passifloraceae)

Passionflowers are semitropical vines that can survive infrequent frosts. Maypop and *Passiflora mollissima*, which are winter-hardy to Zone 6, are the exceptions. The semievergreen to evergreen vines grow from 15 to 80 feet (4.6–24.4m) long. They will easily overgrow an area, but can be kept within bounds by firm annual pruning to retain the open habit that is conducive to flower production. Passionflowers require full sun and do best in a sheltered location, thriving in most garden soils.

These vines, including such edible varieties as maypop (see Passionfruit, page 65) are grown for their amazingly beautiful, complex flowers. Passionflowers were named by the Spanish missionaries working in the New World tropics, who saw the flower parts as symbols of the Passion of Christ, representing the crown of thorns, hammer, and nails used in the Crucifixion, and other theological images. However symbolically you want to see them, passionflowers are absolutely gorgeous, with wide-open petals that reveal colorful filaments (which indeed look like the crown) and other structures.

P. caerulea, one of the hardiest of the passionflowers, is a woody climber that grows to about 15 feet (4.6m) tall. The showy, 4-inch (10.2cm) flowers, bossed with blue filaments, can almost cover the plant, producing a breathtaking effect. Egg-shaped, yellow fruit follow the flowers. 'Constance Elliott' is one of the best-named forms, with fragrant white flowers. *Passiflora × alatocaerulea*, a fragrant hybrid, has white and pink flowers with a purple, blue, and white crown. *Passiflora manicata* is a fast-growing, vigorous vine, with a profusion of bright red flowers with a blue crown. *Passiflora racemosa*, with its deeply lobed leaves, is considered the most appealing of the red-flowered species of passionflower.

Porcelain Berry

Ampelopsis brevipedunculata (Vitaceae)

Native to northeastern Asia, this vigorous, tendril climber can grow to 20 feet (6.1m). Porcelain berry is hardy in Zones 5 to 8. Often mistaken for a wild grape, its trilobed leaves resemble grape leaves. In fall, the foliage turns a lovely shade of scarlet. The flowers are insignificant; however, the berries are quite unusual. Borne in clusters in late summer and early fall, the berrylike fruit start out yellowish-green and mature to different hues of blue with a unique crackled effect that resembles fine porcelain. Eventually the berries blacken. Be forewarned: this vine has naturalized in many areas and is considered an invasive weed by some gardeners. Once you have a porcelain berry vine in your garden, it is very difficult to get rid of. The cultivar 'Elegans', with lovely variegated leaves, is much better behaved and highly recommended for planting.

Porcelain berry grows almost anywhere, which is a good part of the reason it has been relegated to weed status. It thrives in full sun to partial shade, and in any type of soil. To grow an exceptional porcelain berry vine, plant in well-drained, humusy soil. Porcelain berry can easily cover a barn if provided with support. Try to plant the vine where you can get close enough to appreciate its charming fruit. Train it up the posts of a porch, where you can keep a watchful eye on it. Prune in early spring to thin and shape the vine. Head it back to keep it within bounds.

PORCELAIN BERRY

Scarlet Clematis

Clematis texensis (Ranunculaceae)

A Texas native, scarlet clematis is hardy in Zones 4 to 10. One of the showiest species, it bears 1-inch (2.5cm), scarlet, bell-shaped flowers that start blooming in July and continue until the first frost. The seedpods that follow resemble silvery plumes. This quick-growing clematis can climb to 10 feet (3m), making it an excellent vine to train along a low fence or post. It is relatively drought-tolerant, but prefers regular watering. Hybrids include 'Comtesse de Onslow', with scarlet-banded, violet-purple flowers; 'Duchess of Albany', with brown-centered, pink flowers; and 'Etoile Rose', with cerise-pink flowers edged silver. See Clematis (page 89) for cultivation tips.

Silver Lace Vine

Polygonum aubertii (Polygonaceae)

A twisting vine, silver lace vine (also known as fleeceflower) is hardy in Zones 5 to 10. It climbs quickly to 25 feet (7.6m), with wiry intertwining stems. It is best known and prized for its abundant bloom. In late summer continuing into autumn, small greenish-white flowers billow along the tops of the branches in 6- to 8-inch (15.2–20.3cm) panicles. Providing beauty at a time when so much else in the garden has passed its prime, this flowering vine makes a great end-of-season show. In areas with cold winters it is deciduous, in milder climates evergreen. In spring the glossy new leaves are pale green, tipped red. They are distinctively arrow-shaped with wavy edges. It quickly hides a fence or covers an arbor.

Plant in full sun in most regions, but give it partial shade where the summers are hot. Silver lace vine thrives in most soils and is drought- and pollution-tolerant. During the summer, water deeply once a month and the vine will thrive. Tie the branches of silver lace vine to a support to train young plants.

SILVER LACE VINE

Silver Vine

Actinidia polygama (Actinidiaceae)

Male plants of the silver vine, a native of east Asia, are grown for the green leaves that are tinged silvery white. It is more vigorous than kolomikta vine

(to which silver vine is related), growing to 25 feet (7.6m) or more. Fragrant, 1-inch (2.5cm) white flowers with brown or yellow anthers are often hidden by the luxuriant foliage. Cats are drawn to this vine as they are to catnip. When planting silver vine, give some thought to protecting the young vine from marauding felines by screening with chicken wire or hardware cloth. The young stems must be anchored and trained to climb. Once the plant is well established, it can hold its own against a cat. In Japan, the leaves and

salted fruit are considered a delicacy. See Kolomikta Vine (page 103) for cultivation tips.

Star Jasmine

Trachelospermum jasminoides (Apocynaceae)

Native to China, star jasmine is one of the most widely grown vines in North America, particularly the United States. Its popularity in the South is evidenced by its other name, Confederate jasmine. This evergreen, weakly twining vine is a great addition to any landscape in Zones 8 to 10.

Star jasmine will grow to 20 feet (6.1m) and is handsome both in bloom and out because the oval, glossy, dark green leaves are attractive even when unadorned with the vine's charcateristic blooms. The 2- to 3-inch (5–7.6cm) star-shaped flowers have slightly twisted petals arising at the end of short tubes. Fragrance from the blooms perfumes the air from early May until midsummer, attracting bees and butterflies. The sprawling, supple branches give rise to the different "looks" this vine can take, depending how it is grown—a sprawling ground cover spreading 4 to 5 feet (1.2–1.5m), an elegant frame for an entryway, or a living screen grown on a fence. It climbs happily up a trellis in a narrow space; grown in a pot, it can look like a cascading small shrub. (In fact, the 'Variegatum' type has lovely green and white variegated leaves and is hardier than the species, both of which characteristics make it even more shrublike.)

Star jasmine grows equally well in sun and shade, preferring moist, well-drained soil of any type. Fertilize in early spring and again in late summer to promote healthy growth and good foliage color. Keep well watered through the spring and summer; do not let the plant dry out. Look for a specimen with long branches to train as an upright vine. In the early stages of training, tie the branches to a sturdy support. Prune whenever necessary to keep the plant in shape. You can shear a vine that covers a fence in early spring or autumn. Prune mature vines annually to encourage new flowering branches, and cut out older woody branches. See also Yellow Star Jasmine (page 115).

Sweet Autumn Clematis

Clematis paniculata (Ranunculaceae)

This clematis, which can grow to 30 feet (9.1m), is prized for its fragrant, 1 to 1½-inch (2.5–3.8cm) flowers that grace the vine from late July to October. Decorative seedpods follow, which can persist well into winter. Hardy to Zone 5, it is evergreen in areas with mild winters. It will handsomely cover a split-rail fence, arbor, or trellis. Be sure to plant it where you can appreciate its sweet scent. See Clematis (page 89) for cultivation tips.

TRUMPET CREEPER

Campsis spp. (Bignoniaceae)

Trumpet creepers are aggressive, deciduous, flowering vines. In midsummer they are in their glory, in full bloom with terminal clusters of six to twelve, brilliant, 3-inch (7.6cm), trumpet-shaped flowers in vivid hues of orange and scarlet. The flowers attract hummingbirds. The vines can grow up to 30 feet (9m), climbing by aerial rootlets that attach their stems to any rough surface.

Plant trumpet creepers in full sun. They prefer rich, well-drained soil and ample water, yet will grow in almost any soil. Support young vines until the clinging rootlets form. The rootlets do not hold tightly to a surface. Heavy winds can separate branches from their support unless well secured. Trumpet creepers are best suited for covering large stone walls, training up the trunk of a large tree, or filling in against a large fence. Beware, the roots send out suckers, which serve to spread the vines quickly over large areas. Cut out the suckers to keep the vines from becoming too invasive. Trumpet creeper, trained from an early age and kept pruned, will grow into a beautiful, large hedge. Prune to reduce the overall volume of the branches; pinch back growing tips of branches to encourage strong growth at the base of branches. See also Chinese Trumpet Creeper (page 88), 'Madame Galen' Trumpet Creeper (page 104), and Trumpet Creeper Vine (page 111).

SWEET AUTUMN CLEMATIS

Trumpet Creeper Vine

Campsis radicans (Bignoniaceae)

Hardy in Zones 4 to 8, the vigorous, native trumpet creeper vine can grow to 40 feet (12.2m). Lovely, 3-inch (7.6cm), orange blooms marked with red flower in mid-July. Five-inch (12.7cm)-long capsules persist through the winter. In areas with freezing winters, the vine dies to the ground, growing again in spring. 'Flava' is a yellow-flowered variety. See Trumpet Creeper (page 110) for cultivation tips.

Trumpet Honeysuckle

Lonicera sempervirens (Caprifoliacae)

Also known as coral honeysuckle, the evergreen to semideciduous trumpet honeysuckle is native to the northeastern United States. Hardy from Zones 4 to 10, it has a lovely open form, producing alluring, 2-inch (5.1cm), coral-to-red trumpetlike flowers in summer. The flowers, which are not fragrant, are followed by scarlet fruit in autumn. The broadly oval leaves are pale blue-green underneath, and join to the stem distinctively at their bases. This is another rampant vine, and it can grow to 50 feet (15.2m) on its twining stems, but more often stops at 25 feet (7.6m). Unsupported, it makes a superlative ground cover, quickly enveloping large areas. It forms an attractive screen when trained on a trellis or fence. Cut back the stems after they bloom or in early spring to control the size of the vine and encourage new branching. 'Sulphurea' has lovely yellow flowers. 'Superba' bears vivid scarlet blooms. See Honeysuckle (page 99) for cultivation tips.

TRUMPET VINE

Distictis spp. (Bignoniaceae)

The robust, evergreen trumpet vines are hardy only in Zones 9 and 10. They can climb 20 to 30 feet (6.1–9m), using clinging tendrils. Blooming from late spring to early fall, they make a bold statement in the garden

TRUMPET CREEPER VINE

with their beautiful 4-inch (10.2cm), red-orange, trumpet-shaped flowes. The flowers are borne on terminal clusters that stand out from the foliage.

Plant in full sun in moist, well-drained, fertile loam. Trumpet vines will grow in partial shade and in most soil, as long as they are not waterlogged. Keep newly planted vines well watered, and feed once in spring, once in summer, and once in autumn. Once the vines are established, feed only in early spring. These vines can readily become top-heavy and benefit from a strong pruning after the flowers fade in autumn; this controls the size of the vines and helps rejuvenate them. Use a high fence, arbor, trellis, or wall to support and showcase the vines. See also Blood-Red Trumpet Vine (page 85) and Vanilla Trumpet Vine (below).

Vanilla Trumpet Vine

Distictis laxiflora (Bignoniaceae)

Plant at the edge of a terrace or walkway, so passersby are treated to the sweet vanilla scent that perfumes the air when vanilla trumpet vine blooms. The 3-inch (7.6cm) flowers open purple, fading to orchid and white before they drop off the vine. In the warmest areas, this vine blooms for as long as eight months. Unlike its relative, the last tendril of the growing shoot of this vine is unbranched. Vanilla trumpet vine is a more controlled vine, needing only light pruning to keep its shape. Keep it protected from the wind. See Trumpet Vine (page 111) for cultivation tips.

VIRGINIA CREEPER

Violet Trumpet Vine

Clytostoma callistegioides (Bignoniaceae)

The robust, tropical, evergreen, flowering violet trumpet vine (also called Argentine trumpet vine or love charm) can grow up to 40 feet (12.2m) high, spreading 15 to 20 feet (4.6–6.1m). Not a vine for the faint of heart, nor for the smallest gardens. It is hardy in Zones 9 and 10. Lavender-orchid blooms cover the vine from midspring to fall, giving it a very soft look, whether it is used as a background or planted alone as a specimen. The 3-inch (7.6cm), trumpet-shaped flowers are borne in terminal clusters. A closer look reveals that they are violet, streaked deep purple to the throat. Although the vine climbs by tendrils, the tendrils are not strong, and need to be attached by other means to its support.

Violet trumpet vine grows in sun or shade. It is adaptable, growing in most well-drained garden soils from clay to sandy. It is pest-free and can tolerate a windy site. Water regularly and fertilize in early spring. It requires strong support for the heavy branches; start training the vine when it is very young. Prune in late winter to remove dead wood, tangled branches, reduce overall volume, and direct growth. Throughout the long flowering season, cut back spent blooms and any overly long branches. Its habit, with long drooping branches, gives it a graceful look when trained to drape over tall fences or the eaves of structures. It works well as a tropical screen on a long fence, especially near a water feature or patio. See Trumpet Vine (page 111) for cultivation tips.

Virginia Creeper

Parthenocissus quinquefolia (Vitaceae)

Many people mistake Virginia creeper for poison ivy, and vice versa. Remember the old adage, "leaves of three, let it be": that is poison ivy. Virginia creeper, a woodbine, is easily identified by its five leaflets, ranging from 2 to 6 inches (5.1–15.2cm) long, with coarsely toothed margins. In early spring, the leaves are tinged purple, then turn deep green. In autumn they put on a magnificent show of bright scarlet color. The summer flowers are insignificant, but the bluish-black berries on red stalks persist well into winter. Virginia creeper needs a rough surface to climb. A vigorous vine, it can reach to 50 feet (15.2m). It is beautiful in a woodland, where the long pendant branches can be appreciated. It also makes an excellent ground cover for slopes, preventing erosion. The stems root wherever they touch the ground, helping to stabilize the soil.

'Engelmannii', Engelmann creeper, forms a dense cover with small leathery leaves. 'Saint-Paulii', St. Paul's creeper, can hold itself up better than the species; it is distinguished by its rounder leaves. Virginia creeper is showy planted against a wall or fence, and is the perfect plant for the shaded arbor or pergola. See Woodbine (page 115) for cultivation tips.

Winter Creeper

Euonymus fortunei (Celastraceae)

An attractive evergreen, trailing vine, winter creeper (also known as American bittersweet) is hardy in Zones 4 to 8. Extremely adaptable, it

'SILVER QUEEN' WINTER CREEPER

thrives in the cold Midwest and the hot, arid Southwest. Winter creeper has rootlike hold-fasts that enable it to climb on any rough surface. Handsome, fine-textured, glossy-green foliage covers the spreading stems. This plant has two forms. As a juvenile, the slender clinging stems have small leaves. An established plant may throw out some mature branches, which are bushy in form, bear inconspicuous flowers and bright red fruit, with larger, leathery leaves. Cuttings taken from mature branches will result in shrublike plants. Prune out mature branches as soon as they appear, if you want to maintain an even look.

Plant winter creeper in full sun to partial shade. It will grow in most soils, equally happy in clay or sandy soil. In the coldest regions, it may sunburn in winter from reflected snow glare; protect it from winter's glare if necessary. The vine roots easily along the stem in any moist, well-drained soil, making it an ideal choice for growing on slopes and controlling erosion. Allow 1 to 2 feet (30.5–61cm) between plants. Mulch well to discourage weeds. Once the plant is established, the dense leaf cover will keep weeds from germinating.

Winter creeper is restrained in its growth compared to most vines, growing only to about 10 feet (3m) after a number of years. For this reason it is well-suited to a low-maintenance garden. It requires pruning in spring only to direct its growth or keep it within desired bounds. It clings, without additional support, to brick, concrete, or wood. It is equally good as a ground cover or trained up a low wall or against the foundation of a house.

A number of choice cultivars are available. 'Colorata' is a good candidate for autumn and winter interest, with green leaves that turn reddish-purple with colder weather. It trains easily. 'Gracilis' has variegated leaves (green with cream) that turn pink as the weather gets cold. It is a slow-growing trailer. 'Minima', also known as baby winter creeper, has very small, ½-inch (1.2cm) leaves, making it a good, fine-textured cover for a low wall. 'Kewensis' is slower growing, with tinier leaves than 'Minima'. 'Silver Queen' is lovely with white-edged leaves. 'Vegeta', a mounding, shrubby form with large leaves, grows 4 feet (1.2m) tall, and can easily cover an area 15 to 20 feet (4.6–6.1m) wide—great for hiding a wall, and especially handsome in autumn, when the orange fruit appear.

WISTERIA

Wisteria spp. (Fabaceae)

Wisterias are the most popular vines, with their dripping panicles of fragrant flowers in spring, and large, sinuously twisting woody vines. Hardy in Zones 5 to 9, wisterias can grow in many places, twining to 40 feet (12.2m) or more. The delicate-looking, large compound leaves are made of seven to nine small, oval, light green leaflets. Their bright color is a contrast to the many deep green vines, giving them a fresh look, even in midsummer. The clusters of pealike flowers come in a range of hues from white to pink to violet. Flower clusters may range from 6 inches (15.2cm) to 4 feet (1.2m) in length, and are followed by velvety, beanlike pods. Wisteria is nothing if not versatile. It is elegant in a woodland, twining up a tree; however, the wisteria will eventually strangle the support tree. Traditionally wisteria are planted on sturdy arbors or pergolas, and is lovely reflected in a pond or pool.

Plant wisterias in full sun in moist, well-drained, humusy loam. They need lots of water when they are in bloom. When grown in alkaline soils, wisterias

WISTERIA

can appear chlorotic, so give an iron supplement to "green up" the leaves. Fertilize with superphosphate in early spring before the buds break, to encourage bloom. Wisterias take several seasons before they bloom, needing to build a storehouse of food before they can expend energy producing flowers. Be patient, for the wait is worth it. Once the plant has begun flowering, prune to keep in shape. Prune after it finishes blooming or in winter to cut down on vegetative growth, thus encouraging later bloom. Cut long back branches to three or five buds. Creative pruning can give the plant a unique form; weave it through a split-rail fence or make a self-supporting tree. See also Chinese Wisteria (page 88) and Japanese Wisteria (page 102).

WOODBINE

Parthenocissus spp. (Vitaceae)

Woodbines are deciduous vines that are highly adaptable. Hardy from Zones 4 to 10, they are good vines for covering large areas. They climb by means of flat, adhesive disks at the ends of branching tendrils. Woodbines are spectacular scaling the side of a building, but are best suited to stucco, stone, or brick as they can damage wood-shingled edifices. In autumn, the leaves give a colorful show in hues of red and gold, before dropping off.

These vines are easy to grow in sun or shade. The preferred soil is well-drained, moist loam, but they will tolerate almost any soil type. Provide ample water throughout the growing season. To cover a large wall, plant the vines close to the support, spacing them 2 to 4 feet (61cm–1.2m) apart. When the vines are young, cut back the stems to encourage branching. For the first year or two, guide the branches up the support. After the vines are established, prune in early spring to keep them within bounds and to guide the growth. See also Boston Ivy (page 85) and Virginia Creeper (page 113).

Yellow Jessamine

Gelsemium sempervirens (Loganiaceae)

The state flower of South Carolina, yellow jessamine (also called Carolina yellow jessamine, Carolina jessamine, Carolina jasmine) is native from Texas to Virginia and hardy in Zones 7 to 10. An open, cascading habit and evergreen foliage make it highly desirable in the garden. Fragrant, bright yellow, trumpet-shaped flowers begin to grace the vine in early spring, lasting into summer in Zones 7 and 8, and persisting into early winter in Zones 9 and 10. In full bloom, it looks like a scented blanket of sunny yellow. It grows to 20 feet (6.1m), with slender, reddish-brown stems that twist to climb. Glossy, 1- to 4-inch (2.5–10.2cm), lance-shaped leaves remain on the vine year-round.

YELLOW JESSAMINE

Plant in full sun to partial shade in any type of soil. It is moderately drought tolerant, but appreciates regular watering. It is fine planted in a breezy spot—the branches sway to and fro in the wind. An easy-to-grow, pest-free vine, it is restrained in its growth. Tie it to a sturdy support when planting. Once mature, prune the vine in autumn, cutting back side shoots to maintain a pleasing shape. You can cut it back severely if it becomes top-heavy. Fertilize lightly twice a year—in early spring and again after flowering. It lends itself to use as an evergreen screen, a handsome solution to shade a patio. It can be grown as a ground cover if kept cut back to 3 feet (91.4cm)—perfect to cover a bank. This vine is versatile, growing happily in a container or trained on a fan trellis. In colder areas, it can be grown as a houseplant. Caution: all parts of the plant are poisonous.

Yellow Star Jasmine

Trachelospermum asiaticum (Apocynaceae)

Native to Japan, yellow star jasmine is hardy to Zone 7. Less vigorous than its white-flowered cousin, it is a good choice for slightly colder climates. The light yellow flowers are very fragrant, blooming from April through June, the wavy petals held erect above deeper, dull green leaves. It grows well in a hanging basket outdoors or in, and makes an excellent ground cover and fence screen. See Star Jasmine (page 109) for cultivation tips.

CHAPTER
5

Vines & Climbers In the Garden

The designs presented in this chapter contain perhaps more vines and climbers than might normally be included in a single garden. In fact, the designs include several plants that aren't part of the A-to-Z section (and several that aren't vines or climbers). Additionally, some of the designs show plants maturing or blooming simutaneously when actually they flower at entirely different points in the growing season. These considerations aside, the idea behind this section is to convey the possibilities for utilizing the beauty and versatility of these plants in any site or location. Moreover, you are encouraged to modify these plans by including preferred plants or substituting cultivars of different colors.

Climbing Roses

Train your favorite climbing or rambling rose along a split rail fence. The result is a soft, country look that also has definite pragmatic benefits—the fence becomes more of a barrier when covered with a thorny rose and the rose itself gets plenty of air circulation, which results in a lower risk of disease.

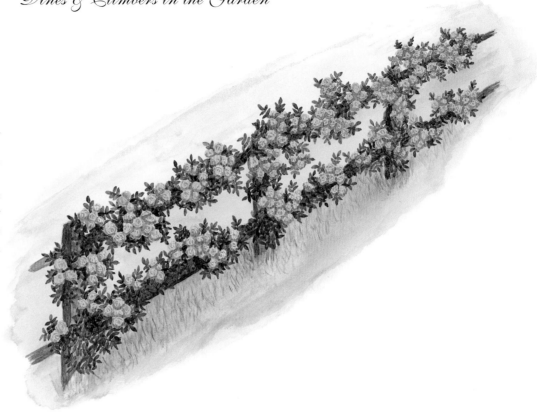

Annuals and Perennials on Antique Iron Fence

This drawing is a bit deceiving, as all the flowers pictured do not bloom at the same time. Instead, you get several seasons of color in a small space. The leopard's bane blooms earliest in spring, followed by the primroses and the pinks. The pinks and sweet peas start to bloom around the same time, and the scents from both are delightful. The calendula and canary creeper bloom almost nonstop throughout the summer, only to be killed by the first autumn frost.

1. *Dianthus* spp. (cottage pinks)
2. *Primula* spp. (primroses)
3. *Calendula officinalis* (calendula)
4. *Doronicum caudatum* (leopard's bane)
5. *Lathyrus odoratus* (sweet pea)
6. *Tropaeolum peregrinum* (canary creeper)

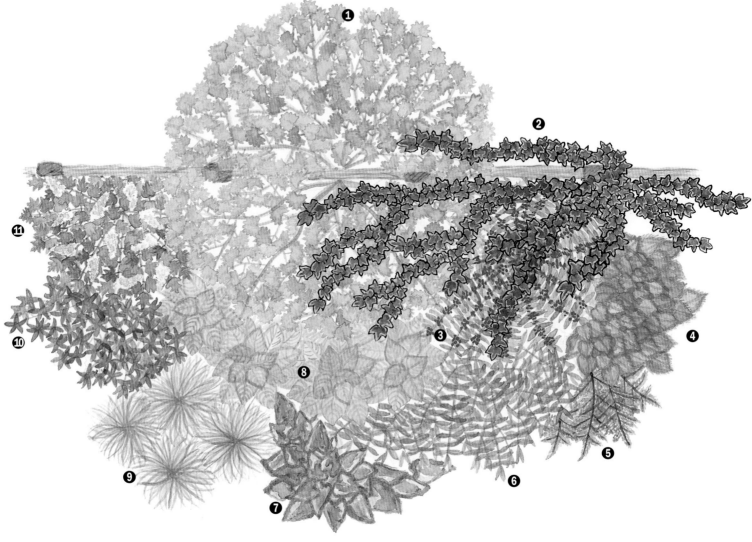

A Variegated Garden in Partial Shade

The maple is the anchor of this garden; the ivy that climbs through the other plants and over the split rail fence perks up the area. A golden glow suffuses all levels of this garden: from early spring, when the full moon maple bursts into leaf, to the fall, when the purple beauty-berry is in full fruit, this garden features wondrous hues. Many of the plants are variegated, adding more subtleties of color. The hydrangea flowers will remain on the plant throughout winter, or you can cut them for use in dried flower arrangements.

1. *Acer shirasawanum* 'Aureum' (golden full moon maple)
2. *Hedera helix* 'Yellow Edge Star' ('Yellow Edge Star' English ivy)
3. *Callicarpa dichotoma* (purple beautyberry)
4. *Ligularia stenocephala* 'The Rocket' ('The Rocket' ligularia)
5. *Athyrium nipponicum* 'Pictum' (Japanese painted fern)
6. *Sarcococca hookeriana* 'Humilus' (sweet box)
7. *Houttuynia cordata* 'Chameleon' (chameleon plant)
8. *Hosta* 'Sum and Substance' ('Sum and Substance' hosta)
9. *Carex morrowii* 'Old Gold' ('Old Gold' sedge)
10. *Skimmia japonica* (Japanese skimmia)
11. *Hydrangea quercifolia* 'Snowflake' ('Snowflake' oakleaf hydrangea)

119

Vining Border for a Sunny Wall

This design, suitable planted against a south-facing wall, combines deciduous and evergreen shrubs with vines, giving a layering effect. The ivy forms a lovely evergreen backdrop, climbing as high on the wall as you wish. The textural mixtures of the plants that support the passion-flower as it blooms through the summer until frost are interesting. This planting has a cool look, with blues, pinks, and purples the most prominent colors. Subtle coloration is noted with seasonal changes. The garden has winter interest, and its peak time is summer through fall.

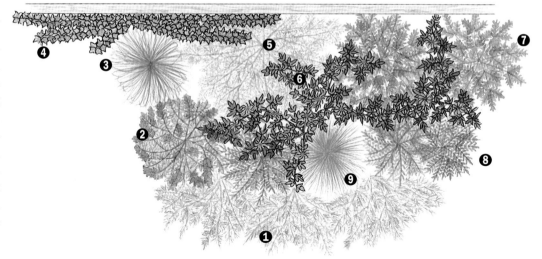

1. *Juniperus horizontalis* 'Bar Harbor' ('Bar Harbor' juniper)
2. *Lespedesa thunbergii* (miyagino-hagi)
3. *Calamagrostis arundinacea* 'Karl Foerster' ('Karl Foerster' reed grass)

4. *Hedera helix* 'Silver Dust' ('Silver Dust' English ivy)
5. *Cupressus* 'Blue Ice' ('Blue Ice' cypress)
6. *Passiflora caerulea* (blue passionflower)
7. *Ilex × meservae* 'Blue Stallion' ('Blue Stallion' Meserve holly)

8. *Itea virginica* 'Henry's Garnet' ('Henry's Garnet' Virginia sweetspire)
9. *Helichotrichon sempervirens* (blue oat grass)

Sunny Location Low-Maintenance Bed

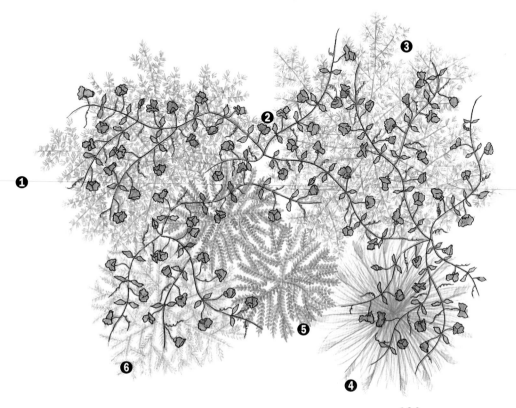

This is a very laid-back bed, where the sweet peas, which with luck will self-seed, are allowed to climb and sensuously drape themselves over the other evergreen plants. The cedars are lovely with their yellow-toned needles, contrasting nicely with the deep purple foliage of the barberry. The plants don't need a lot of attention; given enough space when planted, none will bully its neighbor out of place. The most you'll have to do is cut back the maiden grass in late winter or early spring, after which the new foliage will emerge within several weeks.

1. *Cedrus deodar* 'Snowsprite' ('Snowsprite' deodar cedar)
2. *Lathyrus latifolius* (sweet pea)
3. *Cedrus deodar* 'Kashmir' ('Kashmir' deodar cedar)
4. *Miscanthus sinensis* 'Gracillimus' (maiden grass)
5. *Berberis thunbergii* 'Crimson Pygmy' ('Crimson Pygmy' Japanese barberry)
6. *Picea pungens glauca* 'Montgomery' ('Montgomery' blue spruce)

Golden Bed for a Sunny Location

This sunny bed features overlays of golden foliage, both evergreen and deciduous, while maintaining overall structure. The ornamental grass adds a textural contrast, and tones down the color, especially when it is green. The deep golden flowered vine is allowed to climb gently around and through this bed.

1. *Ilex* × *meservae* 'Golden Girl' ('Golden Girl' Meserve holly)
2. *Eccremocarpus scaber* (Chilean glory flower)
3. *Chamaecyparis obtusa* 'Aurea' (golden hinoki cypress 'Aurea')
4. *Pennisetum alopecuroides* 'Hameln' ('Hameln' fountain grass)
5. *Chamaecyparis obtusa* 'Fernspray Gold' ('Fernspray Gold' hinoki cypress)
6. *Berberis thunbergii* 'Aurea' ('Aurea' Japanese barberry)

Edible Pergola

In a relatively small amount of space, you can grow quite a few edibles—trained upward. This pergola will provide harvest from late spring (peas) through autumn (pumpkins). All the vegetables and fruit are attractive, adding to the beauty of the landscape.

1. **'Sweet 100' tomato**
2. **'Kirby' cucumber**
3. **'Jack Be Nimble' pumpkin**
4. **'Sun Gold' tomato**
5. **Passionfruit**
6. **'Sugar Snap' pea**
7. **Malabar spinach**
8. **Scarlet runner bean**

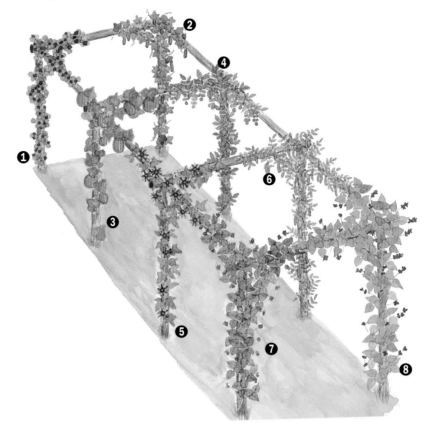

Trellis of Annual and Perennial Climbers

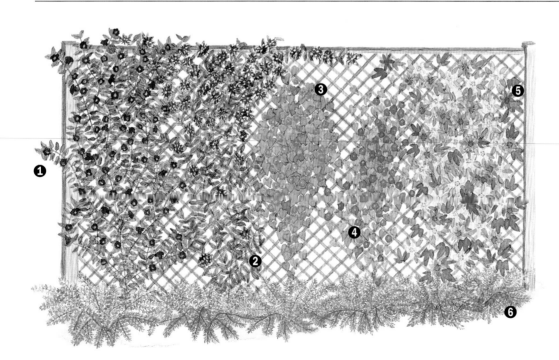

This is a cool screen for a subtropical garden in spring to summer. The cool colors of the blooms are soothing in hot weather. Other varieties of the same plants can be substituted for a hotter-looking garden. In more temperate regions, the blue clock vine and passionflower can be grown as annuals to be enjoyed in one season only, or overwintered indoors so they can be enjoyed year after year.

1. *Cobaea scandens* (cup-and-saucer vine)
2. *Lonicera japonica* 'Purpurea' (purple Japanese honeysuckle)
3. *Ipomoea rubrocerulea* (morning glory)
4. *Thunbergia grandiflora* (blue clock vine)
5. *Passiflora caerulea* mixed with *Clematis montana rubens* (blue passionflower mixed with pink clematis)
6. *Euonymus fortunei* (creeping euonymus)

Vines and Climbers on a Shaded Wall or in a Shaded Walled Bed

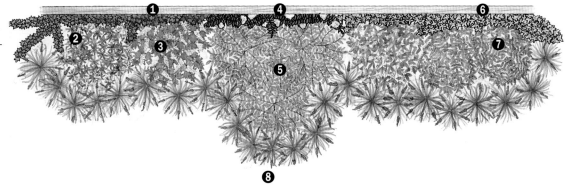

A high wall that shades an area of a garden can be an asset—when you choose the right plants to grow in the shade. The wall pictured is big enough to support three very different vines; with judicious pruning, you can keep each in its own territory or let them intermingle. The color is spectacular when the Boston ivy is in the throes of its autumnal splendor and the lilyturf bursts with spikes of purple bloom. There is much winter interest, too, including the evergreen foliage of the cherry laurel, ivy, and lilyturf. The star of the winter in this arrangement, however, is the red foliage of the dogwood.

1. *Parthenocissus tricuspidata* (Boston ivy)
2. *Pieris japonica* 'Red Mill' ('Red Mill' andromeda)
3. *Hydrangea quercifolia* 'Snowflake' ('Snowflake' oak-leaf hydrangea)
4. *Hydrangea petiolaris* (climbing hydrangea)
5. *Cornus alba* 'Elegantissima' (variegated red twig dogwood)
6. *Hedera helix* 'Buttercup' ('Buttercup' English ivy)
7. *Prunus laurocerasus* 'Otto Luyken' ('Otto Luyken' cherry laurel)
8. *Liriope muscari* 'Big Blue' ('Big Blue' lilyturf)

Vines and Climber Covering a Pavilion

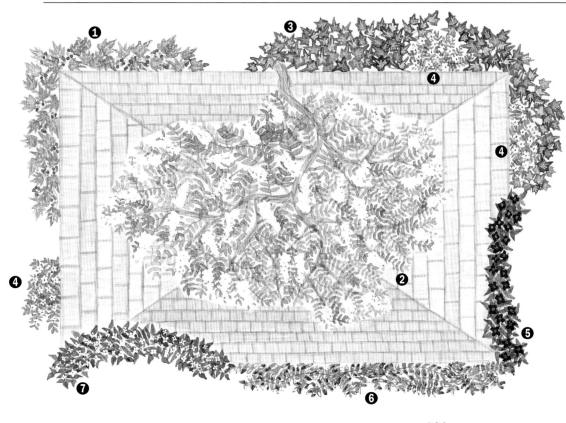

This is a bird's-eye view of a planting that could climb up the posts of a pavilion or a gazebo or even a sturdy pergola (one strong enough to support the weight of the wisteria). Wisteria in winter is leafless but the vine is sinewy and interesting to look at, while the ivy is evergreen, also providing year-round interest. This design is suitable for most temperate areas, though the jasmine (in hanging baskets) is tender and will need to be brought inside before the first autumn frost.

1. *Ampelopsis brevipedunculata* 'Elegans' (variegated porcelain berry)
2. *Wisteria sinensis* 'Alba' (white Chinese wisteria)
3. *Hedera helix* 'Goldheart' ('Goldheart' English ivy)
4. *Jasminum sambac* 'Maid of Orleans' (Arabian jasmine, in hanging baskets)
5. *Clematis jackmanii* (Jackman clematis)
6. *Actinidia kolomikta* (kolomikta vine)
7. *Clematis paniculata* (sweet autumn clematis)

Trellises Tiering a Hillside

This arrangement is designed to dress up a hillside from midspring through fall. The vines are of only two types—honeysuckle and clematis—yet give a wide range of bloom times and brighten the hillside. The plants featured include the early-blooming pink *Clematis montana rubens*, which highlights the vibrant pink bloom of the redbud, and the sweet autumn clematis; the other varieties bloom throughout spring and summer. Blooming late in summer, the ornamental grasses add various shades of green, giving interest to the garden even when the trees and vines are bare.

1. *Hakonechloa macra* 'Aureola' (golden hakone grass)
2. *Liriope muscari* (lilyturf)
3. *Pennisetum alopecurioides* (fountain grass)
4. *Juniperus conferta* 'Blue Pacific' ('Blue Pacific' shore juniper)
5. *Pennisetum* 'Little Bunny' ('Little Bunny' grass)
6. *Molina caerulea* 'Variegata' (variegated purple moor grass)
7. *Festuca ovina* 'Elijah's Blue' ('Elijah's Blue' fescue)
8. *Juniperus scopulorum* 'Moonglow' ('Moonglow' rocky mountain juniper)
9. *Clematis* 'Dr. Ruppel' ('Dr. Ruppel' clematis)
10. *Clematis viticella* 'Etoile Violette' ('Etoile Violette' clematis)

11. *Campsis radicans* (trumpet creeper vine)
12. *Lonicera* × *heckrottii* (goldflame honeysuckle)
13. *Clematis jackmanii* (Jackman clematis)
14. *Lonicera japonica* 'Purpurea' (purple Japanese honeysuckle)
15. *Clematis montana rubens* (pink clematis)
16. *Clematis paniculata* (sweet autumn clematis)
17. *Pinus cembra* (Swiss pine)
18. *Cercis canadensis* 'Forest Pansy' ('Forest Pansy' redbud)

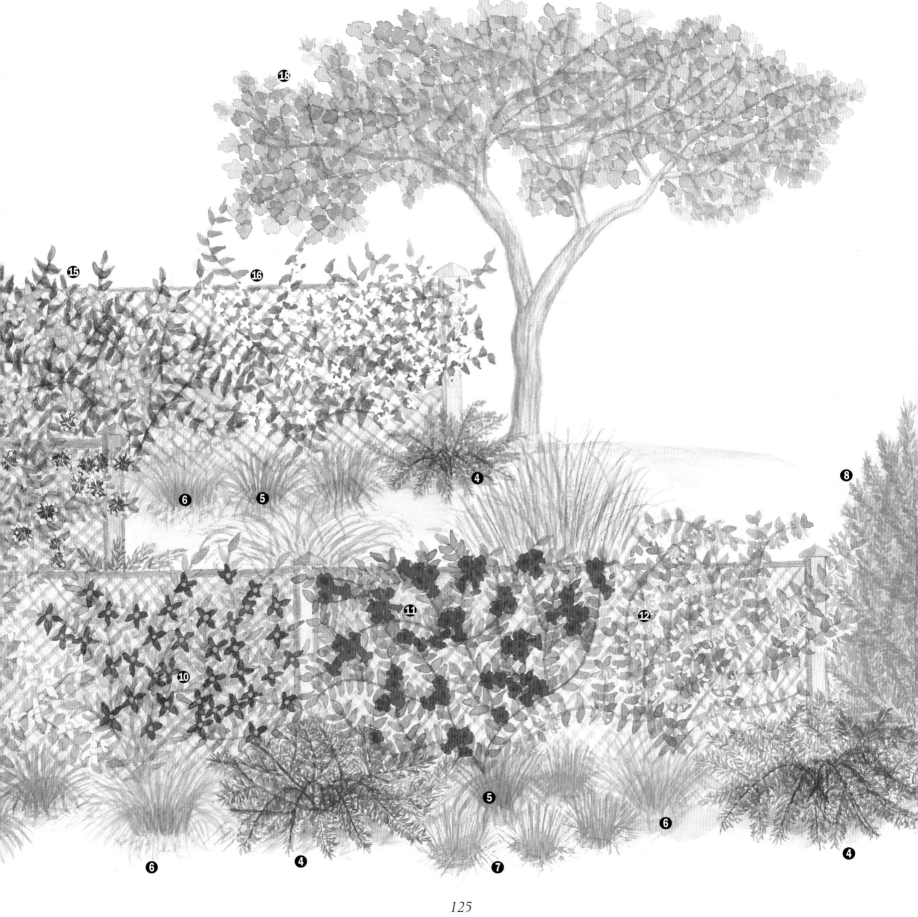

PLANT HARDINESS ZONES

Average annual minimum temperature	Temperature (°F)	(°C)
Zone 1	Below 50°	−45.6
Zone 2	−40° to -50°	−40 to −45
Zone 3	−30° to -40°	−34.4 to −40
Zone 4	−20° to −30°	−28.9 to −34
Zone 5	−10° to −20°	−23.3 to −2
Zone 6	0° to −10°	−17.8 to −2
Zone 7	10° to 0°	−12.2 to −1
Zone 8	20° to 10°	−6.7 to −1
Zone 9	30° to 20°	−1.1 to −1
Zone 10	40° to 30°	4.4 to −1.1

SOURCES

UNITED STATES

Bluestone Perennials
7211 Middle Ridge Road
Madison, OH 44057
800/852-5243

Busse Gardens
Route 2, Box 238
Cokato, MN 55231
612/286-2654

Carroll Gardens
PO Box 310
Westminster, MD 21157
800/638-6334

Donaroma's Nursery
PO Box 2189
Edgartown, MA 21895
508/627-8366

Johnny's Selected Seeds
Foss Hill Road, Box 2580
Albion, ME 04910
207/437-9294

Logee's Greenhouses
141 North Street
Danielson, CT 06239

Merry Gardens
PO Box 595
Camden, ME 04843
207/236-9064

Milaeger's Gardens
4838 Douglas Avenue
Racine WI 53402-2498
414/639-2371

Niche Gardens
111 Dawson Road
Chapel Hill, NC 27516

Nichols Garden Nursery, Inc.
1190 N. Pacific Highway
Albany, OR 97321
503/928-9280

Park Seed Co.
P.O. Box 31
Greenwood, SC 29647
803/223-8555

Seeds Blum
Idaho City Stage
Boise, ID 83706
208/342-0858

Shepherd's Garden Seeds
6116 Highway 9
Felton, CA 95018
408/335-6919

Thompson & Morgan
Box 1308
Jackson, NJ 08527
908/363-2225

Van Bourgondien
PO Box 1000-VC
Babylon, NY 11702

W. Atlee Burpee Co.
300 Park Avenue
Warminster, PA
215/674-4900

Wayside Gardens
1 Garden Lane
Hodges, SC 29695-0001
800/845-1124

White Flower Farm
Route 63
Litchfield, CT 06759-0050
203/567-0801

AUSTRALIA

Country Farm Perennials
RSD Laings Road
Nayook VIC 3821

Cox's Nursery
RMB 216 Oaks Road
Thrilmere NSW 2572

Honeysuckle Cottage Nursery
Lot 35 Bowen Mountain Road
Bowen Mountain via Grosevale NSW 2753

Swan Bros Pty Ltd
490 Galston Road
Dural NSW 2158

CANADA

Corn Hill Nursery Ltd.
RR 5
Petitcodiac NB EOA 2HO

Ferncliff Gardens
SS 1
Mission, British Columbia
V2V 5V6

McFayden Seed Co. Ltd.
Box 1800
Brandon, Manitoba
R7A 6N4

Stirling Perennials
RR 1
Morpeth, Ontario
N0P 1X0